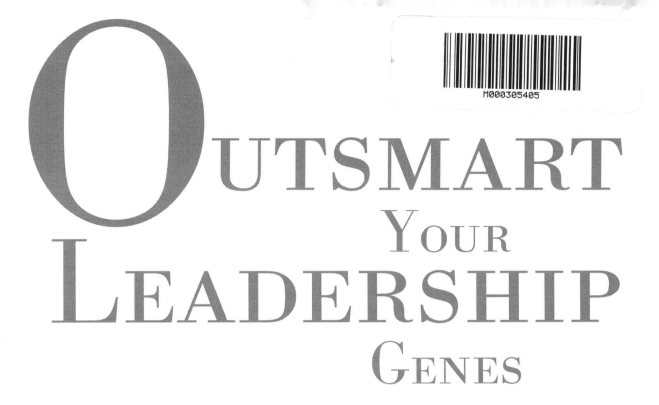

OUTSMART YOUR LEADERSHIP GENES

PRACTICAL PRESCRIPTIONS FOR TODAY'S LEADERS

RENEE B. BOOTH, PH.D.
AND
MICHELE PORTERFIELD

1st edition, September 2013

For permission to copy or share this work, please write:

Leadership Solutions, Inc.
The Bellevue
200 South Broad Street, Suite 405
Philadelphia, PA 19102
215.893.0180
info@leadership-solutions.com
www.leadership-solutions.com

Ordering Information at www.leadership-solutions.com/outsmart

ISBN-13: 978-0615864693
ISBN-10: 0615864694

This book was designed by Mary Helgesen Gabel, Gabel Graphics.
www.gabelgraphics.com
Font is Trade Gothic.
Cover font is ITC Garamond BE and Goudy Text.
Cover symbols are Alana Ornaments.

Dedication

This book is dedicated to our children, Adam Booth, and Alex and Erica Porterfield. They inspire us every day and remind us of how important it is to do what you love and have fun in the process.

Acknowledgments

This book could not have been possible without the support, commitment, and active involvement of a number of people—to whom we owe a very special thanks. Thank you, first and foremost, to the staff at Leadership Solutions, particularly Erica Bennett, Tracy Brown, Bridget Gammage, and Aaron Weiss. You were instrumental in helping keep our efforts on track and were always willing to help with every aspect of the book—from brainstorming to editing to questionnaire development to project management. We are so lucky to be surrounded by such a great team who helps make everything possible. Thank you also to the countless leaders and managers we have worked with over the years. It has been a pleasure to partner with you and we have learned a great deal through the process of coaching you. Our work with you is what truly motivated us to write this book so that we could spread the word to others. A huge thank you goes out to our external partners as well. First and foremost, thank you to Sharyn Kolberg, our writing partner and editor at every step of the way. Your expertise, insights, and encouragement to keep the effort alive in the midst of trying to run the business were critical to getting us to this stage. We are so glad you stuck with us to the end (beginning with our infamous weekend in the Poconos) and we are so grateful to have you as a true partner. A huge thank you to Mary Gabel who got us to the finish line and brought the publication process knowledge to the table. Your professionalism, patience, and expertise are very much appreciated. Lastly, thank you to Bob McCullough and his colleagues at the Gelfond Group for helping us through the questionnaire design process. You know the survey business like no other. And, perhaps it goes without saying, but a big thank you goes out to each of our families and all of our professional colleagues, who always encouraged us to keep at it because they knew it would be a great personal accomplishment in the end.

We are very grateful to have such an amazing circle of family, friends, colleagues, and clients. We appreciate your ongoing support and partnership.

Contents

Why You Should Read This Book

You have probably read your share of books on how to be a more effective leader. We certainly have. Throughout our careers as management consultants and executive coaches, we have been searching for a smart, practical book that helps men and women become better leaders and managers, both for themselves and for those around them. Unfortunately though, most of the books we've found focus their advice and wisdom in a way that seems limiting and not inclusive of all that can be done. More specifically, these books focus on advice about how leaders need to change *themselves* in order to be more effective, without considering other external factors that could actually make a more meaningful difference. We simply feel like something is missing, and this book is our attempt to fill that gap. We believe that more emphasis needs to be put on the *environment* as a neglected element that needs to be added to the conversation. We are surprised by how few leaders consider the environmental component as a powerful tool to enhance their leadership effectiveness, and we wrote this book to offer practical and pragmatic advice in this area. This is not about abandoning efforts to refine your behavioral characteristics, but rather an opportunity to accelerate and complement that process.

Given that you have chosen to read this book, we have to assume that you too are not fully satisfied and are continuing to look for better answers and more pragmatic solutions. Simply stated, most of the available books go into great detail about how you must change yourself—including your values, traits, behaviors, and motives—in order to become better at what you do. Change yourself as a person, they say, in order to become a more effective leader. It seems that the message basically boils down to "the problem is YOU. Change who you are and things will get better for everyone." They tell you that by becoming a different person, you can miraculously morph into a more effective leader.

Of course there may be things about yourself that, with some tweaking, would positively impact your leadership effectiveness. Perhaps you could improve your presentations in front of senior people by speaking more clearly, getting to the point more quickly, and using less technical jargon. Or, perhaps you could be more sensitive to others in meetings by not dominating the conversation all of the time. Our advice is to keep working at these things—they are definitely important. At the same time, though, think of this book as a way to supplement and complement those efforts.

This book is for anyone who is looking for a more workable, practical approach to being a more effective leader. Whether you are a new manager, a seasoned professional, or an aspiring leader who is just getting started, the common-sense solutions you will find here don't require you to change who you are as a person. Nor do they require you to submit yourself to years in therapy telling a stranger your innermost thoughts and feelings, only to end up pretty much the same as you were when you started. We're not saying that you're perfect the way you are and that you don't ever need to change. We're just suggesting that changing yourself, like changing bad habits, is particularly challenging and may take more time than you have, given the realities of today's work environment and the pressure to perform.

Perhaps you're reading this book because you've gotten some kind of feedback that indicates some gaps in your effectiveness as a leader, or maybe you are putting pressure on yourself to change in certain ways because you are ambitious and want to get promoted to the next level. Maybe you are in a job that simply doesn't feel like a good fit, and yet you feel stuck because you don't see new opportunities on the horizon. Rather than convincing you that you need to make sweeping personality changes, this book will help you to discover concrete methods to outsmart your leadership deficiencies by focusing on ways to influence and improve the environment in which you work.

By way of analogy, if you've ever been given a serious medical diagnosis such as diabetes, you know that there may not be much you can do about the genes that may have caused your illness. However, you can make changes (which are not necessarily extreme or complicated) to your *environment* that will override those errant genes and either cure your disease or enable you to manage your symptoms more effectively and live a more satisfying life. If you had diabetes for example, you could help manage the disease by eating smaller, low carbohydrate meals, more often during the day. If you are told that you are genetically predisposed to heart disease, you can make a conscious effort to exercise regularly to get your heart pumping, and eat less salt on your fries. The same holds true for your leadership genes. If, for example, you have a more self-contained style, you could be more careful to hire people who will more naturally bring energy and excitement into your group. Or you could modify the organizational structure around you to ensure that you don't have such a large number of people as direct reports wanting your constant attention and engagement.

The Benefits of Outsmarting Your Leadership Genes

Putting in the effort to change elements of your environment will have far-reaching advantages, some of which are personal, direct, and immediate, and some of which are more focused on others and long-term in nature. We also know that the expectations put upon us in organizations today make it critical that we give ourselves as much advantage as possible. This book gives you the tools you need to access and leverage that advantage.

The primary benefits of looking at leadership development in this new way include:

- **Putting Your Development in Your Own Hands:** You don't have to wait for the organization to produce and offer a comprehensive leadership development program to give you all of the tools and techniques to be effective. You don't need to take a week or more away from work and family to enroll in a university-based executive leadership program. You can take control of things and get to work on developing yourself immediately, without needing approval, resources, or money.

- **Increasing the Organization's Bottom Line:** If you are a more effective leader, your people will likely have higher levels of job satisfaction. Higher job satisfaction leads to increased productivity, and increased productivity has a positive impact on the organization's bottom line. Organizations spend hundreds of thousands of dollars on training their leaders to develop their skills. The question remains though whether they really ever see the return on that investment. Applying the techniques in *Outsmart Your Leadership Genes*, on the other hand, often involves little or no hard cost to the company and this in turn helps the bottom line.

- **Reducing the Stress Factor:** Consistently getting negative feedback creates mental, emotional, and even physical stress. There's a tremendous amount of pressure in today's organizations to produce more and to do more with less in order to remain viable and competitive. The stress in organizations can be overwhelming. That's bad enough. But when you add on the fact that you might not be a perfect match to the leadership requirements of your job, the stress level increases exponentially. When you are trying your best to change who you are, with the inevitable minimal progress, you can't help but feel discouraged and frustrated, both personally and professionally. While this book can't fix the outside pressures you may be facing, it can give you very practical tools and advice to better manage the stress factors that are at play in your day-to-day work life.

- **Creating a Positive Work Experience:** You owe it your employees to be an effective leader and to create a positive work experience for them. If you don't, the most talented people in your department or organization will begin to consider more attractive opportunities, either in other areas of the organization or, worse yet, outside the organization altogether. Then, as a leader, you are left to continually rebuild—something that requires more time, money, and extra effort than would be needed if the staffing situation were more stable. By manipulating factors outside of yourself, you will no doubt positively impact the work experience of your people, and this will in turn impact retention and motivation. We know from research time and time again that a motivated workforce is more creative, more collaborative, and produces better results.

- **Acquiring a Portable Skill Set:** You can take these solutions (or prescriptions as we will refer to them later in the book) with you wherever you go, such as to a new job or organization—in the same way that you can transfer your medical prescriptions to a new pharmacy if you relocate or need to find a more convenient location. Instead of making you dependent on the skills or support of your boss, or the formal training provided by your organization, these prescriptions give you more personal control. They give you the power to make change happen for yourself, and to take such learning and insights with you wherever you may go in your career.

Why We Wrote This Book

Over our years as executive coaches working with hundreds of managers in a variety of organizations and industries, we have come to realize that the leadership challenges faced by people are often more similar than different. The same issues keep coming up—no matter what type of company it is, or the age, race, or gender of the people we are trying to help. The specific situations may be different, but the task for us is always the same: fix what senior executives see as leadership gaps. Senior executives often know they have a problem with one of their leaders, but many of them have no idea how to solve it. They say things like "help make him more confident" or "she needs to be more motivational." As executive coaches, we can only work with a limited number of people. By writing this book, we hope to broaden our reach and give everyone an opportunity to become better at the leadership game. Our goal is to alleviate the feelings of inadequacy and frustration on the part of managers who are told they need to be more effective in some way, without being given any tools to actually make that happen.

In this book we will help you identify your personal leadership tendencies and the aspects of the environment that can be altered to help you be a more effective leader. Just like a doctor who would prescribe medication to help you live a healthier life, we will offer you prescriptions to help you become a healthier leader. This book is not a "how-to" for inadequate leaders. It isn't a "cure" for someone who is ill. It's about making an effective person even more effective. This is not an academic tome that asks you to sit on the couch and analyze your behavior patterns. This is an action-oriented guidebook full of practical prescriptions for improving your work environment, producing concrete results, and moving your career forward. It's a voyage that begins with small steps and continues with concerted ongoing efforts. We invite you to come on this journey with us and become the great leaders we know you can be.

Chapter 1

Prescriptions for Leadership Health

A Tale of Two Leaders

Not long ago, our company was called in by the senior leader of a large healthcare organization in the northeast because he felt like two of his key people, Alex and Erica, were not performing at the optimal level. Some of the issues related to how each of them led their respective teams, and other issues related to them working together effectively as peers. These two people, whom we were told were both high-potential leaders, were somehow derailing to the point that it now got the attention of more senior leadership. "She is over-controlling," said one of the senior people, "and he is inaccessible. These issues are negatively impacting not only their relationship with one another but also the productivity within the division."

First, we spoke to each of the managers to get their take on the situation. Yes, they used to like each other. And yes, they used to work well together. But as time went on, resentments began to build. Alex had made an important decision that Erica felt was hers to make. Erica instituted a policy that Alex felt interfered with his responsibilities. As their relationship deteriorated, the repercussions were felt throughout the organization. Many employees felt like they were left to take sides and were not able to get the resources they needed to meet their goals and objectives. Cross-functional communication became strained and ultimately a major deadline that required coordinated efforts was missed.

In order for us to understand the root of the problem, we had to look beyond the more superficial personality dynamics. Over time it became clear that the situation had less to do with Erica being overly controlling or Alex not being available. While these were undoubtedly contributing to the situation, more involved discussions revealed that what was actually at the heart of the matter was a lack of processes and norms.

We began to work with the two leaders simultaneously to set up new procedures and assign each person specific functions. One such solution was to establish a weekly meeting for Alex and Erica to meet one-on-one. From these meetings, they agreed to send one another project updates so everyone in their respective groups knew what was going on. Additionally, they agreed to facilitate weekly team meetings whereby all of the key stakeholders came together to talk through challenges and address issues. They also established clear meeting norms about what was and was not acceptable behavior. Once they started putting these things in place, they began to realize they didn't have a fundamental relationship problem after all. In the end, the environment was altered by simply adding some structure, clarifying roles and boundaries, and implementing new processes. Along the way, they both learned that the situation was not something to take so personally. While they knew they still needed to keep working on repairing and solidifying their relationship, they could at the same time alter other things in their environment to allow them to work effectively together and create a better work experience for others around them. After several months with the new processes and norms in place, the noise level from those who supported both Alex and Erica quieted down significantly. Staff was able to focus on doing the work at hand without being distracted by questions regarding who was supposed to handle what, or who was supposed to be handed off to whom. Alex and Erica appeared more composed and less frustrated by each other in meetings amongst their peers, and slowly but surely they began getting more comfortable talking openly about challenges in their respective areas without feeling defensive or argumentative. While senior management was not yet ready to promote either of them until they saw more consistent performance over time, Alex and Erica came up much more positively in talent-related discussions and it appeared things were on the upswing.

It has been our experience that very few people are able to fundamentally change who they are in order to become better leaders. Even with the help of successful bosses, other internal leaders, external consultants, workshops, and executive coaches, change remains elusive. Some people even go so far as to work on their own personal time with a psychologist who has a deeper level of understanding regarding human behavior and creating change. Yet, despite consistent and concerted efforts, certain behaviors and approaches simply won't budge.

Is there a better way to approach change in the workplace? We believe so. After more than 20 years of executive coaching, we believe that leaders are better off learning how to use and manipulate key elements of their work environment to minimize personal and professional weaknesses that may be impacting their ability to be fully successful. It is the age-old relationship between nature and nurture. There are some things that are just natural to us as human beings, like being impulsive, introverted, or driven. We call these hardwired characteristics. It's really difficult to change these things about ourselves. Imagine trying to change the way you smile or the way you walk. It's possible, but it sure feels better when you do it the way that you've always done it. We also know, both from personal experience and from working as executive coaches, that when people experience a crisis or come under a great deal of pressure or stress, they can't help but go back to their underlying, natural personality characteristics.

Think of it this way. You go to your doctor and he tells you that your blood pressure is higher than it should be, that it runs in your family, and that your age, sex, and race make you predisposed to hypertension. Your natural instinct is to do whatever you can to avoid developing high blood pressure, but where do you even begin? Would you attempt to educate yourself on gene therapy and try to figure out ways to change your genetic structure? Not likely.

The best way to address your situation would be to figure out how to change your *environment* so that you can circumvent your blood pressure prognosis. You can learn to eat better foods that are low in sodium and fat. You can find an exercise buddy who will walk with you several times a week. You can organize a lunch-time yoga class to help reduce your stress. On your next visit to the doctor you may very well find out that your blood pressure is back in a more normal range. Yet, nothing about your genetic make-up has changed. You have simply *outsmarted* your genes by using the support that your environment has to offer to undermine the negative effects (see Figure 1).

Figure 1

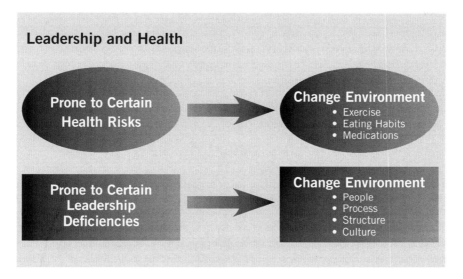

In fact, each of us can outsmart our leadership genes - those hardwired characteristics that can get in the way of us galvanizing, motivating, and providing strategic direction as leaders. We simply need to learn the key environmental interventions that are related to each of our particular leadership ailments. In this book, you will find specific and practical prescriptions that will allow you to *outsmart your leadership genes.* These prescriptions have been developed based on real life experiences working with organizational leaders who have become disheartened and discouraged after years of searching for new strategies to enhance their effectiveness by trying to change themselves. It is not necessary to spend time wondering if you were born with the "right stuff" to be a leader. Each of us, no matter what personality traits we were born with, can be empowered to become effective leaders if we take full advantage of the environment around us.

The Psychological Impact of the Environment

It is easy to overlook the impact that our environment has on our lives. We establish routines for ourselves and then follow them blindly. We decorate our homes and offices and then never give them another thought. We accept certain aspects of our personal and work lives as being simply "the way things are." Yet, in doing so, we create a vicious cycle for ourselves because it is precisely these environmental influences that can be used to our advantage.

There is a well-known tenet within industrial psychology that says you can alter the environment in which people work, and it will change the experience that everyone has in that environment. For instance, if you change the color of the paint on the walls and reorganize people's desks to a new configuration, it can lighten the atmosphere and help your staff work together in a different way. You can relocate your office to a space that gets much more natural sunlight to lift people's spirits. This doesn't negate the fact that people may still need to change some things about themselves, but it does suggest that the environment can help put people in a more positive frame of mind to make those changes. In other words, let the environment in which you work help you be better at what you do.

Think about music, for example. If you are in a bad mood, put on your favorite type of music and see how quickly your mood changes. Your favorite rock band might get you revved up to think of the next great idea. Classical music might help you feel calm so that you can be more thoughtful and reflective about a sticky situation at the office. Try going to a group exercise class. No matter how reluctant you may be to participate, as soon as the music starts your body automatically starts moving to the beat, and your state of mind gradually transitions to a much more positive place. You didn't change yourself, but the environment changed you.

Making the Difference

Sometimes, when things go wrong, we want to blame the organization or the particular position we hold; we imagine that if we just manage to land the perfect job we will be set for life. We're inclined to jump ship, thinking life will be new and different if we go somewhere else. And then we land that great job and discover we're the same person; the same set of circumstances unfold, and we're faced with the same struggles. That's because we're being shortsighted about it. Don't jump the gun and think that by virtue of a new organization it will all somehow be different and better. We should instead be making changes in the current environment to achieve the results we want.

To illustrate the point, let's consider Naomi Clayton. Naomi is the head of the legal department of a hospital system, and a consummate introvert. She really doesn't like to talk a lot, explain things to others, or get involved with the personal lives of her employees. It's not that she doesn't like people, it's just that the amount of time she needs to spend with her group to make everyone feel connected is exhausting, time consuming, and sometimes simply boring. She has found great ways to avoid this connection. She keeps her door closed most of the time and has learned to avoid eye contact when walking by others in the hallways. In addition, when others come into her office to speak with her, she continues to work on her computer, as if she can listen with one ear and continue correcting reports while her employee is sitting there.

Naomi got away with this kind of behavior until the company decided that every manager was required to participate in a 360° evaluation process. Needless to say, the feedback on Naomi wasn't glowing. The employees felt that Naomi didn't really like people. Even worse, they didn't think she had the potential to improve. Worried, Naomi asked her boss (an easy-going, friendly senior executive with an open door policy) for help. He was happy to provide specific recommendations that he had used successfully in his own past.

Based on the feedback, Naomi went to her boss and asked for his advice. Without much hesitation, he told her that it was important for her to work on being "more likeable," and that in doing so others would view her in a more positive light. Naomi listened to what he said because she knew he was very well regarded as an effective leader, but at the same time she left having absolutely no idea how to actually do what he has asking her to do. When she went to him the next week to get advice about some specific strategies to pursue, her boss suggested that she begin by starting each conversation with some small talk that would make others more comfortable and allow them to get to know her on a more personal level. He suggested she speak much more openly on topics such as her kids and her family, about which she had many interesting stories. Naomi was skeptical but willing to give it a try. During her first few weeks she felt awkward and disingenuous, and her employees appeared visibly uncomfortable. After a few short months, she heard through the grapevine that her employees dreaded running into her in the hallways because they knew they would have to engage in a contrived and awkward conversation. This not only hurt Naomi's feelings, it also made her feel even more alienated from those who worked for her. In truth, Naomi was an interesting and caring person, but she was also very private. She felt betrayed by her employees for giving her such negative feedback after having worked so hard to protect and support them over the years.

It seemed that the forced small talk was actually making things worse. Naomi wanted to be viewed as one of the future leaders of the organization and knew that she needed to find a more workable solution. While she understood that her boss meant well, she also knew that she needed to get a different perspective and more expert advice. She went back to her boss after a few weeks and tactfully asked for an executive coach to help things along. The formula she was using was not doing the trick.

Naomi + Personality Change = Frustration and Failure

When we first began coaching Naomi, we told her that she should stop engaging in the small talk efforts. Her unsuccessful efforts to change herself had been causing her much angst and frustration, not to mention concern about her long-term prospects to advance her career.

We told her that while there were personality issues that she might want to address, there were other options to help her improve her leadership impact. She was immediately relieved to discover that she could take meaningful actions without leaving her comfort zone. We suggested that we look at her work environment to identify specific strategies to outsmart her leadership deficiencies. Naomi, a logical and thoughtful individual, realized that for years she had ignored that very important ally in her leadership development—her environment. We outlined what we thought were appropriate elements of her work environment to which she could make changes and modifications. Instead of beating herself up for getting such challenging feedback, we spoke about how she could improve the situation by making changes to her organizational structure, processes, departmental roles, and cultural norms.

Over the course of our time together, we collaborated to identify specific prescriptions based on her 360° feedback. Naomi began to develop a meaningful and practical plan of action. She implemented a variety of environmental changes - some simple and some more complex—that made a major difference in her leadership impact. For instance, she changed the frequency and design of her staff meetings. She instituted her own reward and recognition program to ensure that staff members who went the extra mile were acknowledged.

She hired a Chief of Staff with a particularly outgoing personality and made it part of this person's role to make sure that any team issues were addressed in a timely manner. Naomi also instituted a book club whereby her staff came together monthly to engage with one another about a current business topic.

None of these prescriptions required Naomi to become a different person. She simply focused on outsmarting her leadership genes to become a better leader—which ultimately produced better business results. The next year when Naomi received her 360° feedback, her scores were greatly improved. Her employees reported that they felt more connected to her, to each other, and to the team. Naomi was, of course, excited by the new feedback. More importantly though, she also realized how much more relaxed and comfortable she felt not having so much stress and strain associated with trying to be the perfect leader. Her boss was very encouraging as well, and made special mention in her performance review that the year had truly been transformative for her and her development within the company. Her formula had changed:

Naomi + Environmental Change = Success

When Naomi tried to change her personality by making small talk to get others to like her more, all she accomplished was more alienation on everyone's part. When she focused on changing her environment instead, she was able to produce much better results. And in the process, she too began to change, slowly but surely becoming a bit less introverted and better able to develop healthy relationships with her people. She did not have to wait for a miraculous transformation to occur. Without even realizing it, she was improving herself along the way in a natural, sustainable manner. At the same time she was able to positively affect the morale of her team and ultimately the results of the company.

What We Mean by Environment

There are four basic areas included in our definition of **environment.** We recognize that environment can be defined in many ways, but our focus is on the specific environmental elements that we know most managers and leaders can actually impact. You will learn more about the factors in the following chapters, but here they are in a nutshell (see Figure 2):

Figure 2

You and Your Environment

- **Structure:** The way in which you structure the organization around you, including such things as reporting relationships, span of control, and job design. For instance, if you are a person who tends to get too involved in your staff's personal lives, a prescription in this area might be to minimize the number of direct reports you have so that you have fewer people to attend to on a day-to-day basis.

- **Processes:** The way in which you manage information to produce desired results, including such aspects as communication, meeting management, and decision making. For instance, if you are a manager who is strong at motivating people but needs help on the more operational elements of your role, one prescription might be to ensure that a specific portion of each of your staff meetings is dedicated to having direct reports provide status reports on key projects so that everyone is clear about progress on key initiatives and accountability. Another prescription might be rotating the management of the meeting to each of your direct reports.

- **People:** The way you utilize the talent around you to get the optimum results, including such issues as hiring certain kinds of people, and establishing unique roles for people so that they can complement your style. For example, if you are someone who focuses mostly on the content of the work and less on whether or not people are feeling particularly motivated, you might benefit from putting a few people on your staff in charge of coming up with specific recommendations for motivational activities such as teambuilding events for the staff. Another idea is to have a small group of direct reports operate as the culture committee, focused on staying in touch with how employees are feeling and initiating events and experiences intended to keep people feeling positive even in challenging times.

- **Culture:** The way it feels to work in your department, including cultural norms (e.g., collaborative, open to differences, entrepreneurial, etc.). For instance, one prescription for a leader who has a reputation for being rigid and overly structured in his/her personality might be to allow people who perform at a certain level a degree of flexibility to work from home or work flexible hours so that they can attend to the other demands of their lives. It is a simple change in the culture that undoubtedly will have people talking less and less about the rigid and inflexible boss.

This book describes a number of key leadership styles that have consistently emerged in our coaching practice. For each of these leadership styles, we have identified a series of prescriptions that will help leaders outsmart the frequently observed deficiencies associated with the style. We are confident that you will find yourself in one or more of these styles, and our hope is that you will be open to making the environmental changes identified so that you can maximize your leadership impact and live a more productive, successful, and stress-free work life.

A MOST IMPORTANT NOTE

None of the five leadership styles is the "ideal" to make a good leader. What we do know about leaders though is that they are effective in five fundamental areas. A good leader:

- Motivates people
- Produces high quality results
- Builds strategic relationships and works well with others
- Has a vision for the future
- Is intellectually strong and makes sound, rational decisions.

Knowing that all of us have certain natural strengths, weaknesses, and preferences, this book is about trying to help you be effective across ALL of these important areas, so that you can maximize your impact.

The next chapter will explain the mechanics of how to use this book. You will also find a questionnaire that will help you determine which of five leadership styles describes you best. These styles may feel familiar to you, based on other tools and instruments you have taken. These styles are simply our way of delineating the different personality types, based on work with real people in real organizations. And, while you may have seen or read about versions of the leadership styles before, the prescriptions you will find in each chapter are what make this book different from the others you may have read.

Chapter 2

How to Use this Book

Now that you have an idea of what this book is about and what it can do for you, it's time to put the ideas into action. This is not a book that you just read and then ponder for a while until you decide whether you want to adopt some of the ideas. The hope is that you will utilize it more as a practical workbook from which you can identify specific plans of action that you can implement in short order and, in most cases, without a whole lot of effort or resources.

In order to get the most out of what is offered in the book, the following steps are recommended:

Steps to Make the Most of this Book

1. **Find the style that fits:** Fill out the questionnaire to determine which leadership style(s) best describes you.

2. **Get to know your style:** Read through the chapters that pertain to your dominant leadership styles to better understand the strengths and downsides. You may find that you have a dominant style and a close backup.

3. **Check out the prescriptions for your style:** Read the prescriptions suggested in that chapter and select those that resonate with you the most, based on your own unique circumstances.

4. **Consider your prescriptions in context:** Take your particular context and circumstances into consideration, so that your good intentions don't go awry.

5. **Test the waters:** Test out the prescriptions in your particular circumstances. Amend them as needed to get the desired results.

6. **Go deeper:** This section contains a broader perspective to help you understand how you are likely to react in certain typical events in the work environment. Consider this information to more effectively navigate within your situation.

Staying with the medical metaphor, reading this book is like going to the doctor. You know something is wrong, but you're not quite sure what it is. The best thing about the process of outsmarting your leadership genes is that you are your own doctor. You can make the diagnosis immediately upon answering the questions, finding the prescription(s) that fit best for you, and beginning to work on the cure today. You can customize your prescription as needed, once you get a personal sense of what is working for you and what might need some adjusting (see Figure 3).

Figure 3

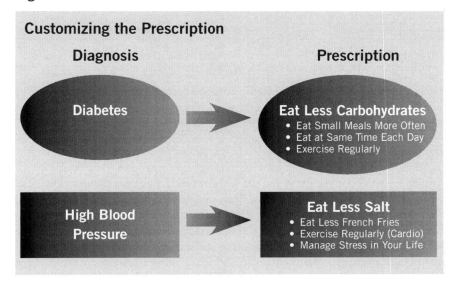

Customizing the Prescription

Diagnosis	Prescription

Diabetes → **Eat Less Carbohydrates**
- Eat Small Meals More Often
- Eat at Same Time Each Day
- Exercise Regularly

High Blood Pressure → **Eat Less Salt**
- Eat Less French Fries
- Exercise Regularly (Cardio)
- Manage Stress in Your Life

The Leadership Style Diagnostic

This questionnaire below should take you no longer than 10 or 15 minutes to complete. The questions in the tool are based purely on our practical experience working with leaders, rather than any scientifically valid research study. Don't get bogged down in details or over-think your answers. Use your instincts and go with your gut. For each statement, identify the extent to which the behavior is descriptive of your behavior, values, and way of thinking.

LEADERSHIP STYLES QUESTIONNAIRE

First, read through the entire list of 30 statements. Then, indicate the extent to which each statement describes you. While it is not a requirement, the results will be most helpful if you try to have some balance in your responses, according to the following distribution.

Great Extent (3) = Select 10 statement
Some Extent (2) = Select 10 statements
Little Extent (1) = Select 10 statements

It is likely easiest to first choose the statements that describe you most (Great Extent), followed by the statements that describe you least (Little Extent). The remaining statements likely fall in between (Some Extent). Don't overthink your responses since there are no right or wrong answers, but try to be honest about yourself.

Place your answers in Scoring Sheet table on the final page.

	Please indicate the extent to which each statement describes you.	Little Extent	Some Extent	Great Extent
1.	I compete with other individuals to be recognized as the best	1	2	3
2.	I feel bored by things like project plans, details, and implementation	1	2	3
3.	I feel that it's very important to create a nurturing work environment	1	2	3
4.	I think it's more important to work with technically competent people than people I get along well with	1	2	3
5.	I believe everyone should be held to the same standards with no exceptions	1	2	3
6.	I seek tangible evidence to demonstrate that I'm ranked #1 among my peers	1	2	3
7.	I prefer to think about future opportunities rather than current issues	1	2	3
8.	I prefer for my team to operate like a family	1	2	3
9.	I believe that any activity that takes me away from focusing on my area of expertise is a waste of my time	1	2	3

	Please indicate the extent to which each statement describes you.	Little Extent	Some Extent	Great Extent
10.	I believe that people should accept their assignments, without much questioning	1	2	3
11.	I think that getting the job done well is ultimately the only thing that matters	1	2	3
12.	I think that frequent risk taking is essential to job satisfaction	1	2	3
13.	I think it is important to know people very well to work effectively together	1	2	3
14.	I seek to identify the right answer no matter what it takes	1	2	3
15.	I regularly follow up with others to ensure accountability and follow-through	1	2	3
16.	I am willing to disregard formal ways of getting things done if I have a better method	1	2	3
17.	I believe good ideas are worth pursuing, even when they seem impossible	1	2	3
18.	I feel ambivalent about delivering difficult feedback, because I worry that the recipient will take the criticism personally	1	2	3
19.	I think when goals are clear, smart people should be able to manage themselves without much direct supervision	1	2	3
20.	I always try to deliver precisely what was asked of me even when it doesn't make perfect sense	1	2	3
21.	I am known for achieving more than was previously thought possible	1	2	3
22.	I like to shock people with my bold ideas	1	2	3
23.	I believe that a manager should protect his or her team from the crossfire	1	2	3

Please indicate the extent to which each statement describes you.	Little Extent	Some Extent	Great Extent
24. I like to work on solving complex problems alone	1	2	3
25. I create rules and processes for myself and others to follow in order to ensure consistency	1	2	3
26. I believe that my job is to drive people to achieve results, even if it means being demanding	1	2	3
27. I try to inspire and motivate during my presentations	1	2	3
28. I believe that it's a boss's responsibility to ensure that people feel happy at work	1	2	3
29. I am the "go to" resource to others for answering challenging questions in my area of expertise	1	2	3
30. I prefer predictability and dislike surprises	1	2	3

Scoring Sheet

Use the space below to record the numerical response you selected for each item.

Remember to aim for some distribution between your ratings of 1, 2, and 3.

A	B	C	D	E
Q. 1 _____	Q. 2 _____	Q. 3 _____	Q. 4 _____	Q. 5 _____
Q. 6 _____	Q. 7 _____	Q. 8 _____	Q. 9 _____	Q. 10 _____
Q. 11 _____	Q. 12 _____	Q. 13 _____	Q. 14 _____	Q. 15 _____
Q. 16 _____	Q. 17 _____	Q. 18 _____	Q. 19 _____	Q. 20 _____
Q. 21 _____	Q. 22 _____	Q. 23 _____	Q. 24 _____	Q. 25 _____
Q. 26 _____	Q. 27 _____	Q. 28 _____	Q. 29 _____	Q. 30 _____
Score: _____	Score: _____	Score: _____	Score: _____	Score: _____

Your total scores will indicate which different leadership styles are most descriptive of you.

Leadership Style Diagnostic Summary of Results

Add up the total in each column to identify your total score for each of the styles. Write your total score in the table below. Identify your dominant and back-up styles by indicating where you received the two highest scores. These are considered your Primary and Secondary Styles.

SCORING SHEET FOR LEADERSHIP STYLE DIAGNOSTIC

Style Category	Your Total Score (from questionnaire)	Primary and Secondary Styles (indicate 2 highest scores)
A. Olympian		
B. Energizer		
C. Guardian		
D. Guru		
E. Stabilizer		
Total Score		

Determining Your Style

Now that you have completed the diagnostic, take a minute to review the summary descriptions of each of the five styles:

Style	Summary Description
A. Olympian	An achievement-oriented manager who is focused on surpassing expectations and driving hard for results.
B. Energizer	A motivational manager who is energized by spreading ideas and galvanizing others around new possibilities.
C. Guardian	A people-focused manager who strives to create a positive environment that is calm and harmonious.
D. Guru	A highly knowledgeable expert who focuses on the content of the work and providing best-in-class expertise.
E. Stabilizer	An administrative manager who follows through as expected by emphasizing consistency, discipline, and accountability.

Don't try to guess which style you think will make you the best leader. There is no judgment here, as no one style is better than another. Every style has its pros and cons, strengths and weaknesses. No one should take the quiz and feel "Darn! I'm an Olympian and I wish I was an Energizer" or "My boss is a Stabilizer—since I want to be in his position I should be a Stabilizer too." It doesn't work that way. You are what you are, but your personal tendencies should not stop you from being an effective leader.

Depending on your personal preference, you might choose to go directly to the chapter that pertains to your dominant style and start identifying particular prescriptions to implement. Or you may choose to skip the diagnostic questionnaire altogether, read through all of the style descriptions to get a better feel for which suits you best, and then identify appropriate prescriptions. We recommend you start with your Dominant style. Read through the chapter describing the style and its attributes in more detail, being brutally honest with yourself about how you really do operate as a leader. Remember, each of the styles has key strengths and downsides. If your dominant style doesn't resonate, read through the style that had the second highest score (and so on) until you get to the style that makes the most sense to you. If you honestly don't see yourself in any of the styles (which rarely happens), or if two styles are closely tied and you can't decide which one is dominant, ask your boss, colleagues, or close friends and have an informal discussion about how they would describe you.

The Prescriptions

Once you know your dominant style, you can turn to the relevant chapter. In each of these chapters you will find a general description of the style, a real-life story illustrating how a leader with that style usually functions within an organization, and examples of how that manager might be able to outsmart his or her leadership genes. The next part of each chapter includes examples of prescriptions for minimizing the challenges that this particular type of leader might encounter. These prescriptions describe specific ways you can make changes to your environment to help you override your ingrained leadership genes and develop a more effective, productive team and workplace.

In each section, you will find several prescriptions and areas of advice. Obviously, we could not include every possible prescription or cover every possible situation that might arise. Instead we chose a select few prescriptions that have been time-tested and proven effective in a variety of industries, cultures, and organizations. These are the prescriptions that we feel provide the most potent medicine. And the truth is that most people can't handle more than a few changes at any one time anyway.

We suggest you read through all of the prescriptions first and then choose one or two that you can begin implementing immediately. Try the one(s) that resonate most with you. If your first strategy doesn't prove to be effective after some reasonable period of time, move on to the next choice. Imagine again that you have gone to your doctor and been diagnosed with high blood pressure. The doctor may prescribe a particular medication, but then suggest that you try meditation or yoga as well. If the first medication doesn't work, you may go back for another. You may try yoga and decide it just does not work for your lifestyle. You may instead commit to listening to calming classical music in the car on the way to and from work (instead of the daily news which can be overwhelmingly negative and bring on more stress). By using one or more of these prescriptions, you may find that your blood pressure returns to normal.

Once you have chosen a prescription, you may also want to turn to Chapter 8 to help you implement it effectively. In this chapter, you will find a worksheet to help you determine the resources you need and what kinds of questions you need to answer before you can implement a prescription (e.g., whether or not a particular prescription is culturally acceptable in your organization, or whether you need your boss's approval to make the change).

Six Easy Steps

So that's it. In just six easy steps, you are on your way to being a more effective leader and increasing your job satisfaction as well as the satisfaction of those around you.

SIX EASY STEPS TO FOLLOW

1. Determine your leadership style
2. *Read the chapter that describes your style*
3. *Read through the prescriptions offered and select ones that fit*
4. *Analyze the issues that need to be considered in implementing your chosen prescription*
5. *Modify prescriptions as needed*
6. *Read through the "Wisdom" section at the end of the chapter*

You've already completed step number one by filling out the leadership style questionnaire. Now it's time to go on to step number two. While you're reading about your style, remember that not everything in the description may fit you perfectly. Even so, keep reading and you will probably recognize enough characteristics to keep you in that category. Then you can try the appropriate prescription(s) that will help you outsmart your leadership genes.

Chapter 3

The Olympian
Winning is Everything

Are you an Olympian type? Start by taking a few minutes to complete the following brief symptom questionnaire.

Please read each of the following statements. Using the scale provided, rate the extent to which each symptom describes you. Total your score by adding up your ratings on individual items. Determine the extent to which this leadership style is reflective of your tendencies based on the final scoring provided.

Rating Scale

1 = This statement hardly describe me
2 = This statement somewhat describes me
3 = This statement definitely describes me

	Please indicate the extent to which each statement describes you.	Little Extent	Some Extent	Great Extent
1.	I compete with other individuals to be recognized as the best	1	2	3
2.	I seek tangible evidence to demonstrate that I'm ranked #1 among my peers	1	2	3
3.	I think that getting the job done well is ultimately the only thing that matters	1	2	3

4.	I am willing to disregard formal ways of getting things done if I have a better method	1	2	3
5.	I am known for achieving more than was previously thought possible	1	2	3
6.	I believe that it's a boss's responsibility to ensure that people feel happy at work	1	2	3
	Total Score			

Total Score	Description
16–18	This is very likely your leadership type
12–15	This may be your leadership type, but you likely demonstrate other types as well
6–11	This is not likely your leadership type

Ron's Story

When Ron was a young boy he would watch his sales executive father and his friends discuss their sales quotas and the amazing trips and other prizes they would win. Ron felt energized just hearing them talk. As a high school and college student, Ron joined the basketball team, debate team, and track team. He kept a journal of his goals and wins and analyzed them to correct any mistakes or lapses in performance. He won many awards and received much recognition. During a college break, Ron went on a rock climbing trip and became completely enthralled. The incredible amount of positive recognition he received by striving and being better than the rest was a powerful motivator for him. When it became difficult to keep up with rock climbing in a regular way, Ron took up running. He trained hard regularly and ultimately began running marathons. His times improved with each and every race, but Ron continued to push himself harder and harder until he set the record in his age group at a well-known, nationally recognized marathon.

When he finally got the opportunity to work in a large, successful company, Ron believed he knew what it took, and he was going to make the best of every chance he was given. He believed his desire to win in sports could bring him nothing but huge advantage in the workplace.

As he himself expected, Ron was eventually hired at a Fortune 100 consumer products corporation and was quickly promoted up through the ranks, from sales representative to sales supervisor and manager to marketing manager, and now as director of sales. Even though he was married with several children, he was committed to devoting whatever time was needed to ensure his success. He believed that working long and hard would ultimately be appreciated by his wife and family, since it was what afforded them the chance to live a good life. Over the years he won a number of awards and special recognition, having garnered a reputation among the senior management as being the ultimate "rain maker." He could sell anybody anything. He was brought into a number of situations where it was necessary to turn things around, and while people had mixed feelings about his methods and unbridled energy, Ron got the job done every time, and he continued to get raises and new opportunities to shine.

Ron was recently asked to make a lateral move to be a Director in the marketing department of the organization in order to improve short-term results. Ron was told that it was a situation that really needed attention because there were productivity issues, low morale amongst the staff, a variety of operational issues, and several processes that needed a real overhaul. In the first six months, Ron worked with his boss to identify and agree upon clear goals and objectives. He did what he did best. He worked harder than ever and expected others to do the same. After just a short time, marketing productivity was up. However, Ron did not feel the familiar rush of adrenalin that came with his success in the past, nor was he being recognized by others as being the best. In staff meetings with his direct reports, he often sensed skepticism and lack of participation. In meetings with his boss and peers he felt as if he was being judged and coming up short. Some of his relationships with his peers began to feel strained. To make matters worse, relationships at home began to get a bit rocky as well. He and his wife had several difficult conversations about the pace and style of their lives, and she told him frankly she thought things were headed in the wrong direction. This got Ron's attention.

Ron asked for feedback from his boss because he wanted to know what was required for him to be exceptional again. Satisfied with the fact that things were improving, Ron's boss remained complimentary, if vague, in his feedback. Ron decided to ask others he worked with what they thought. What he found was interesting. First, he was given credit by all for being smart, productive, and well intentioned. However, because he did not concentrate on operational excellence within his department, it often took more time and energy from others to make things happen. A few people indicated that Ron did not spend enough time building relationships with his peers and didn't coordinate his efforts effectively. Sometimes the decisions he made in his department adversely affected the efforts of others. He took for granted that everyone else would happily sacrifice their personal lives to do whatever it took to surpass expectations. Even though he had solicited the feedback himself, it was a lot for Ron to digest.

After several months, Ron's boss asked him to put together a strategic plan for the marketing group. Ron found it challenging to find time for this, since the immediate needs for increasing productivity seemed much more pressing. Just a few days before he was due to present his initial plan to senior management, Ron took a few hours to put together a presentation outlining what he saw as the appropriate direction for the department moving forward in the next two years. He had planned to interview other key stakeholders and to do external competitive analysis, but somehow time got away from him and such inputs were never incorporated.

A few days after his strategic plan was presented, Ron's boss, Francisco, called a meeting with him. This meeting went very differently than Ron had anticipated. Francisco shared that upper management felt the strategic plan was underdeveloped and off the mark –particularly given the shifts in other parts of the organization. Ron left the meeting feeling completely exhausted and deflated. How, after working so hard and doing exactly what he was asked to do when he came into the role, could he have gone so wrong on what seemed like a simple presentation? Could he recover from what appeared to be a big misstep in the eyes of senior management?

The boss explained that all was not lost—that this was just the initial meeting and that subsequent meetings would create opportunities for him to show more of his true capabilities. He sent Ron on his way and told him they could talk again in a few weeks.

Understanding the Style

As an Olympian, you help organizations move the bar regarding performance. You dare the organization to believe that it can do better than it has ever done before. As a leader, you provide clear and direct feedback and hold others accountable for their performance. You expect those who work for you to be self-motivated and low-maintenance. You will remove barriers to make sure your people can focus on results. You provide your staff with clear goals and objectives and create a very specific language regarding success. You want each person who works for and with you to clearly understand what is expected and the importance of exceeding those expectations. Being critical of others who don't go the extra mile is a hallmark of Olympians. You want others to know where you stand, and will provide staff with frequent and consistent feedback so that they can correct their performance quickly if it is beginning to slide.

Olympians are competitive people who are motivated by doing things better than everyone else. For example, if you're in a sales job, you want to be number one, not just in the top ten percent. In a marketing job, you want to dominate with market share rather than just have strong market positioning. In a staff role such as Finance or Human Resources, you are constantly looking for ways that things around you can be improved—perhaps to save money or accomplish something more quickly.

Olympians set goals that to some might seem unlikely to achieve. Your goals are more challenging than stretch goals, even unrealistic at times. You believe that along with lofty goals come big rewards.

You are known to take the long shot and bet it all if you believe you can exceed expectations—you want to go beyond even when you are already the best. You are singularly focused and persistent despite adversity and obstacles. Some might say you are obsessed with being the best. Your competitive nature transcends all environments and you can't turn it off.

When you are successful, you are often rewarded by being given more latitude and tolerance. In your zealousness to be the very best, you may ignore organization processes and systems and are often known for being tough on relationships. You are not particularly well known for developing talent –instead you see staff as a means to an end. You may only respect certain types of people whom you view as equally competent and ambitious, being unforgiving to those with wildly different personalities or strengths.

You feel justified in not following standard processes if you believe that such processes are bureaucratic and will get in the way of achieving maximum results. You may ignore things such as completion of expense reports or other administrative reporting requirements because you see them as interfering with precious time that could be spent accomplishing more productive tasks. You don't always make the time to train, coach and mentor others properly. In addition, because you are so busy achieving, you are often inaccessible to your staff and others with whom you work. This can lead to confusion and to others actually missing their target performance goals because you were not available to answer questions, resolve conflicts, or provide a forward thinking point of view. You don't necessarily micromanage, but you are a perfectionist who often gets other people to manage the details.

In addition, you are often unaware of deficiencies in your people leadership capabilities. You may not, for example, know when your people are feeling overloaded and need additional resources. Finally, because you are moving so fast and are so focused on achievement of outcomes, you are not particularly good at developing thoughtful processes for such things as communication and decision making.

As a result of the tangible success that you usually produce, however, you are often promoted to a leadership position as a reward.

Unfortunately, the very characteristics that make you successful can ultimately interfere with you becoming a successful leader long term.

Olympians think that the solution to most business problems is for others to work harder at what they do and strive to be their best. You tend to think less about the future than you probably should, and have the potential to be blindsided by long term events or shifts. This is because you are more naturally wired to focus on exactly what is in front of you. Practically speaking, many extreme Olympians never think about things such as what they will do in retirement, because they are so focused on achieving for today. They can't imagine doing anything else but what they are doing now. For some, this makes for challenging times later on in life when it is necessary to let the next generation take over.

When it is brought to your attention that in addition to results you must focus on other aspects of your leadership role, you see this as an opportunity to show that that you can meet the challenge. However, you are quickly bored with the day-to-day tasks and soon supervising staff and such things fall by the wayside. That may be because you are not particularly motivated by developing and mentoring others. You like people and can be particularly persuasive and influential, but you prefer to focus on the work more than any relationship-building activities.

You value people who challenge you. If you should get a "young buck" on your team, you may view this as an exciting contest and be happy to take it on. You prefer to deal only with people you recognize as a fellow Olympian; you don't have much interest in developing your staff to be great down the road. You do just enough to ensure harmonious relationships with your staff, but not much more. In addition, while you understand the importance of the team meeting together, you are likely to use those meetings to inspire and motivate others to perform, rather than to understand the day-to-day issues and challenges facing the staff, or to discuss more strategic oriented topics. You are best when you can have "a hands-on" approach to achieving results. The ultimate conflict for you is how you can continue to be considered for broader leadership responsibilities, even though you are most naturally energized by achieving personal results. If you don't begin to broaden your leadership repertoire, you will find yourself passed over for promotional opportunities and feel outdistanced by peers who have a more balanced leadership style. Of course, this will cause you discomfort because you really want to be nothing less than the very best. You may begin to look around at peers who have progressed to bigger and more influential jobs within the organization, and start to question whether you are becoming obsolete or stale. If overlooked for a promotion, you may be told that it is because you are so valuable in your current role. Yet, you don't feel valuable at all.

The organization is in a dilemma when it comes to Olympian leaders. In the early years of their careers, Olympians provide reliable, exceptional results with minimum oversight. Senior leaders are reluctant to move them because they don't want to experience the inevitable drop in performance that follows their departure. At the same time, senior leaders recognize that without promotional opportunities, Olympians will never get the breadth of experience that will be required for them to function effectively in broader leadership jobs over time. The challenge for you is to reframe and redefine what exceptional performance really means. You need to be sure you can focus on motivating and galvanizing others while demonstrating thoughtfulness about long-term direction and what the future holds. If you can do these things in a deliberate and meaningful way, your chances of continued career progression are much greater.

Summary of the Style
Strengths

- Consistently produce exceptional results
- Focuses on flawless execution in the short term
- Often relied upon under challenging business circumstances
- Sets high expectations for oneself and of others

Challenges

- Limited focus on the future
- Limited focus on relationships, including developing and motivating others
- Poor attention to cultural norms and organizational politics
- Too much focus on "doing" and less on "thinking"

Prescriptions for Olympians

If the story and/or the descriptors of the Olympian resonate with you, consider the following prescriptions as practical tactics and approaches for outsmarting your leadership genes. Review the list in its entirety first, then go back and consider the relevance and appropriateness of each particular item. Make notes in the margins to indicate which of the prescriptions might be worthwhile to incorporate into your plan.

LEADERSHIP PRESCRIPTIONS FOR THE OLYMPIAN

Environmental Element	Prescriptions To Consider
Structure	• **Delegate supervisory responsibilities:** It is essential that the people under your direction get sufficient and meaningful guidance and professional development. Consider identifying someone within your group who can more easily (and naturally) fulfill that responsibility on your behalf. This could be a permanent job or simply a more informal role that a particular individual plays for your group. • **Identify a formalized strategic planning team:** Consider developing a small strategic planning team that meets regularly to ensure that you stay focused on strategic issues and not just the next short-term goal to be accomplished. Putting this structured group in place will ensure that the long-term thinking elements of your job get the appropriate amount of attention and focus regularly. • **Appoint a lieutenant:** Create a role that is responsible to help manage the day-to-day operations associated with running your area of responsibility, as well as to address motivational and developmental issues that arise. The person chosen for the role needs to be a style that balances out your Olympian nature. Specifically, your lieutenant can help ensure that you are not driving your people too hard, make sure that the departmental culture is positive and motivational, and that you are not overly focused on only achieving short-term results.

Process	• **Make staff meetings thought provoking and strategic in nature:** Your formal staff meetings should focus on a broad combination of topics that affect your department's success - not limited to tactical discussions of project updates and specific progress against goals. Consider an agenda that allows staff to express critical issues facing the department today and in the future. Ask your staff to provide you with feedback about what should be on the agenda. Invite guests from other departments to present to your team on ways that you can work together more collaboratively. Also, consider discussing current topics that are facing your industry. Perhaps presenting a new strategic topic periodically will force your staff to think longer-term about issues that will need to be addressed and opportunities you want to exploit. Be sure to make these meetings collaborative and ask for ideas and feedback from your team. Use your one-on-one meetings with staff members to deal with individual performance issues or performance against objectives. • **Push down decision-making authority:** Take inventory of decision-making authority under your sphere of influence, making sure that decisions are truly being made at the lowest level appropriate. This will leave you with more time to focus on the broader issues and decisions that need to be made. Find opportunities to share some of your workload with others and delegate important and meaningful work to them. • **Create your vision with others:** Instead of telling your staff your vision, make the process collaborative and leverage the expertise and insight of your entire team. While it may need to be done in a facilitated fashion by an outside party, the goal is simply to create an experience that will bond people together around something in which they all have a vested interest. Olympians don't naturally focus on such intangibles, but they are critically important to getting maximum motivation from others.

Process (cont'd)	• **Utilize a process for making key decisions:** Because you are action oriented, your instinct may be to trust your gut and make decisions based on what seems right to you—even if you don't have enough information. It will be helpful for you to slow down and reflect before making decisions where possible, and to weigh all of your options and any feedback you have received regarding the issue. Develop and formalize a process which outlines the key steps you will go through before making decisions of any significant consequence. The process should include steps such as data gathering, thorough analysis of multiple options (including pros and cons of each), testing draft ideas with key experts, talking through long term implications of decisions, etc. Most importantly, it will be critical for you to balance your desire for expediency in favor of taking the time to weigh the situation and possible outcomes, both short and long term.

• **Look for ways to reward your people for things other than getting results:** Consider rewarding efforts that are aligned with broader organizational goals and long term objectives, rather than always rewarding others for achieving immediate project outcomes. Doing so will help your direct reports understand the importance of linking their individual effort to those that support the organization as a whole. For you, the focus on rewarding for progress against longer term goals will help you stay more oriented toward more strategic outcomes instead of weekly, monthly, or even quarterly business results. |

Process (cont'd)	• **Meeting management:** Consider incorporating the following prescriptions into how you plan and run your meetings:
	
	  o Introduce thought provoking questions and concepts that are not easily answered by the hard and fast numbers related to your business.
	
	  o Encourage joint problem solving to help ensure inclusiveness and promote learning about how success is achieved.
	
	  o Let other people run your meetings periodically.
	
	  o Invite guests from other departments to gain a broader perspective on the business.

People	• **Develop the members of your team in a balanced way:** Review the talent you manage and take note of whether or not you are providing developmental opportunities to your team in a fair and balanced manner. As an Olympian, you may find yourself focused on the development of other Olympians on your team, since they reflect your values and way of doing things. Using a more structured process like a talent review (facilitated by someone externally), you can guard against a natural inclination to favor development of those who are in your own likeness—and instead learn to develop talent in a more strategic manner. • **Engage yourself with other senior leaders:** Commit yourself to getting to know the senior leaders in your organization as a way of keeping up-to-date on the current thinking and long-term direction of the organization. This can be accomplished by making yourself more available for ad hoc committees that may set policy for the entire enterprise (e.g., human resources, diversity, space planning, business development, etc.). Keep in mind that you will not be able to sustain the relationships if you approach this in a superficial way. You will need to make the time for building and maintaining relationships by actually rolling your sleeves up and working together on issues of importance.

Culture	In addition to the norms that are naturally aligned with the Olympian's strengths, you should also consider emphasizing the following set of norms within your team: • **Thoughtfulness:** Strive to balance the value of "doing" in order to achieve tangible outcomes with the importance of "thinking" to ensure multiple angles have been considered. As an example, allow yourself and your staff time to be thoughtful and take your time to think complex issues through before jumping to immediate conclusions and implementing specific plans. This may mean that certain issues take longer to resolve, but very possibly with better long-term outcomes. • **Winning Through Others:** Strive to create a culture whereby success is defined as achievement of goals via many people's contributions (versus just individual contributions). Make it a point to celebrate group successes when you bring your team together. • **Collaboration and Inclusion:** Work hard to ensure that multiple people are included in key decisions. This will help bring balance to your natural inclination to take everything on and do it all yourself. Additionally, the team will begin to feel like their opinions and perspective truly matter—something that ultimately leads to a deeper level of commitment and a more motivational climate. • **Honest Dialogue:** Create a norm whereby individuals are encouraged to share their opinions about issues openly and honestly, without fear of repercussions. Make sure that others are valued for their opinions, even if they are radically different from your own. • **Tolerance:** Aim to demonstrate a level of authentic patience for people and their differences and levels of proficiency. Examples include tolerating those who are learning from mistakes, letting people talk their ideas through, asking questions of others to fully understand their ideas and perspectives, etc.

Ron's Story Continued

Once the initial sting from the negative feedback wore off, Ron called upon an old mentor from way back. The mentor had since retired, but was still doing selective consulting assignments. Ron explained that while his initial presentation of the strategic plan did not go well, he thought he might have a chance to recover in the next round of presentations. However, he needed some help. Ron's mentor advised him to draw on the richness of the experience around him, instead of just hunkering down to do the work himself because it seemed like the most efficient approach under the circumstances. He reminded Ron that strategic planning was more an exercise in thinking, not doing. Also, he got Ron to think of the situation as more of an opportunity to showcase his broader capabilities to senior staff so that they could view him as more than just a very capable guy who could deliver immediate results.

After a few more conversations with his mentor, Ron summoned a meeting of his direct reports and asked them to provide their input on the future direction of the business. In particular, he tapped into a few people who had a great deal of experience from other organizations and were known to be top notch in their areas. Since the next presentation was not due for another month, Ron appointed a small team of people to do an analysis of the competitive landscape, and to report their findings to the larger group. In the meantime, Ron made a personal commitment to interview several internal stakeholders who could articulate how they anticipated things looking different in the future. That way, Ron could begin thinking about the implications for his area of responsibility. He was frustrated by all the time it took to do the interviews and synthesize the findings, but he knew it was his only chance of recovery. To be sure that all the day-to-day work was kept on track while he focused on this critical project, Ron gave certain people under him decision-making authority regarding issues that he himself would typically have supervised. This made them feel valuable, challenged, and most of all trusted.

At first, the shift was very challenging and Ron felt less of a sense of personal satisfaction, but he trusted his mentor's advice and stuck with the plan. Things got a bit easier each week, and when the various groups and individuals shared their findings and observations, Ron felt much more at ease. The team planned an all-day work session a few weeks prior to the second round of meetings with senior management to piece together all that they had learned and to formulate a comprehensive presentation. Realizing his own natural tendencies, Ron brought in an outside facilitator to help the group make sense of all they had learned, and to develop a cogent and crisp presentation. In an organized fashion, they debated alternative strategies and the pros and cons of each before arriving at a direction that everyone felt comfortable would be the optimal solution.

With each day that passed, Ron gained confidence that he could recover nicely on this one. He discovered significant things that he could collaborate with others to get accomplished—and that success and satisfaction could come from a new source. He came to appreciate that it was just as much about his approach and how he worked with others that actually made him successful. He learned that by depending on others in significant ways, the outcome could actually be even better than he had imagined.

Wisdom for Olympians

It is challenging for you as an Olympian to be seen differently by senior leaders in the organization. Once your reputation as an Olympian has been firmly established, it is difficult for others to see you as a broader leader. Changing others' perspectives takes time and requires the help of those who work for and with you. By following your prescriptions, others will be able to articulate the ways that you have enhanced your business environment and their overall work experience. If you find it impossible to change long-established perceptions, do not hesitate to practice your new approach in other non-work environments such as community or non-profit boards, associations, etc. If you find it impossible to overcome a long-standing reputation inside the organization, you may find it necessary to seek a new opportunity elsewhere, someplace you can have a fresh start and bring your new-found insights to bear so that you can be viewed as a more balanced leader.

As a leader, you are likely to be faced with unique challenges and dynamics in navigating your way through classic leadership responsibilities and particular leadership events. Like many things in life, if you are insightful about how you typically respond to certain situations, you are in a much better position to self-manage in a way that will allow you to be most effective. What follows is specific advice for Olympians for the following situations:

1. *Making an Impact as a Leader*
2. *Managing and Developing Others*
3. *Relationship Building*
4. *Getting Promoted*
5. *Moving On from the Organization*

Making an Impact as an Olympian

Making an impact is about getting yourself and your work noticed in the organization. It is about developing a positive reputation in the minds of others as someone who has the wherewithal to make things happen and improve the organization and its people in some way. Olympians are often challenged in particular ways in this area.

As an Olympian, you always like to feel that you are deep in the trenches and that you are making a direct impact on the work that is being done. However, you need to be able to devote time to motivating and inspiring others, navigating organizational dynamics, and most importantly, thinking about the future. Work hard to balance the time you spend doing hands-on work with providing the leadership that your organization needs. Initially, it may feel as if you are not making a contribution; you may not feel as energized and engaged as when you were producing tangible results. That will pass. Once you reframe your success as getting things done through others you can find great satisfaction in motivating and leading your team. Over time you will grow to value the effort you spend on understanding organizational politics and dynamics because you will begin to see this effort as a strategy for getting things done rather than as a hindrance to your job. Also, the time you spend building strategies and talent for the future will enable you to leave a far more lasting impact on the organization than your individual achievements ever could.

Managing Others as an Olympian

A key element of any leadership role is that of managing and developing talent, and each style is challenged by different aspects of this area of responsibility.

When you're an Olympian, you automatically work faster than most other people. You have always achieved exceptional results by maintaining your razor-sharp focus. At the same time, you can change your course of action on a dime if you feel that things are not working as well as you would like—which is great for you but not so great for the people who work for you. Managing and developing others is likely a particular area of weakness for you. People who work for you are likely to feel that they are walking on eggshells—constantly wondering whether they are good enough in your eyes. Despite good intentions, your Olympian-type behavior can feel unsettling for those around you. If people feel on edge, they are not likely positioned to do their best work. Be careful that your intense focus on delivering results does not blind you to the fact that people working for you may be feeling undervalued and unable to reach their aspirations. If they don't feel like their talents and skills are being fully utilized, high potential people working for you may decide that they are simply not going to get what they need from you—and make choices to move on.

As an Olympian, you are usually better with more seasoned employees than you are with younger, newer hires. You often leave "average" people behind and are not able to harvest their potential. These people may be trying to do their best for you, but they are less and less motivated the more they feel like there is no way they can keep up. It's important for you to view developing others as a "watch and learn" experience. Slow down and give people time. Development doesn't happen overnight. Include your direct reports in as many work situations with you as you can. They will learn plenty from observing your work habits, and you just might gain some insights from them about how to improve your people skills.

Building Relationships as an Olympian

Building and maintaining productive working relationships is a key ingredient for the success of every leader and manager. Technical expertise and smarts are in many ways a foregone conclusion. Here is some perspective about the typical dynamics Olympians face in developing effective relationships, and some practical advice and guidance to help things along where needed.

Because of your need to exceed targets or perform better than expected, others may think that you are using them just to ensure that the job gets done. That is not a good foundation for relationship-building. You want people to feel that they are collaborating with you and that it is worth *their* while for you to be successful. Olympians often feel that have to compete with everyone. It is critical to believe at a fundamental level that people are your most valuable asset—not a hindrance to your successful performance. You want the people you work with to be on your side. The best way to achieve this is to show them visible signs of your appreciation.

Getting Promoted as an Olympian

Each style has a unique set of dynamics when it comes to trying to get promoted and dealing with the realities of not having received the promotion. Here are a few pointers for Olympians.

It is important for you to be patient. Often times, promotions come later than you think they should. This is partly because getting a promotion is a very tangible and visible way to know that you have succeeded—something that Olympians in particular live for day in and day out. Your natural instinct is to push for the promotion as soon as there is even a slight possibility that it might be a good fit for you. Your accomplishments are often the most visible and measurable in the company, and you are often rewarded for these results. As such, you may push to be promoted because you feel you have the evidence to prove your worthiness. In fact, you may not have paid enough attention to things that are not visible and are more difficult to measure, like composure, looking out for others, and being more team-focused. These are all things that will likely matter to those making the decisions.

Olympians are prone to statements like, "My promotion is long overdue. I'm invaluable to this company," or "I should be running my own company in five years." There are many examples of people who have said these kinds of things and been very successful. But it doesn't work for everyone or in every company. Some organizations have had problems because a young Olympian has been promoted without the seasoning, life experience, and insights to be an effective leader. When that person does not succeed fully in the larger role though, it is much harder, both for the person and the organizational leadership, to go back and reset the pace all over again.

There are many more examples of successful people who got promoted later than they thought they should. In fact, many successful executives were surprised when they were promoted because they were having such a good time working in their current position. Instead of focusing on the obvious outcome of a big promotion, they focused on their work and had challenging and satisfying roles as their real priority. While this mindset may require patience for the Olympian, the outcome is far better in the long run.

Additionally, the less you talk about wanting to get promoted, the better off you will be. Believe it or not, most bosses are keenly aware of who wants to be promoted. They get their information from a variety of sources and observations. Don't let your ambitions get the best of you. If you don't get a promotion, keep in mind that how you respond to the situation can definitely affect future promotions. Be a class act. Give yourself time to settle your emotions down, then talk with your boss to better understand why you did not get the job. Take the time to listen carefully, since subtleties may not be your natural strength.

Moving on as an Olympian

At some point or another in your leadership career, you may find yourself having to move on from an organization. If so, the following insights and advice may be meaningful to ensure that you are able to keep things in a healthy perspective.

As an Olympian, you have a tendency to want clear indications that it is time to move on. For a variety of different reasons, organizations do not always want to provide such clarity. If you do not get the answers you want, you may be too quick to consider other options. It is this impatience that often leads Olympians to leave their organizations for opportunities that may be less than ideal in the long run. You need to spend the time and research required to determine the nature, size, and scope of your next opportunity so that you don't jump into a bad choice—which may ultimately require another job transition sooner than you anticipate. If you find yourself wondering whether it is time to go, first ask for the clarity that you need. Be mindful though that if you take the risk to bring it up overtly you may get a truly honest response. If you don't get the clarity you need and your instincts still tell you to move on, take your time to ensure that the next move you make is the right one for the right reasons.

Ron's Story Continued

When it came time to present the second time around, Ron felt much better prepared. He realized over the past few months all that he had missed and now could bring to the meeting in terms of insights and proposed plans. Before the actual presentation, Ron met briefly with his boss to review what he was planning to present so that he could be sure things were much more on track.

After the presentation, Ron went back to his team and thanked them for all that they had contributed to the final outcome. Later that day he ran into a Vice President, one of the more senior people who had heard the presentation. The Vice President commented on what a great job Ron had done. He was very impressed not only by the thorough analysis, but even more so by the fact that Ron reached out to many others in order to build his plan. The Vice President indicated that some of those people who Ron had reached out to had shared some unsolicited feedback about Ron and how great it was to work with him.

Ron reflected a lot on his experience with this strategic planning process. While it was painful at first, he knew that the experience was impactful and helped him to realize that what had made him successful in his career to date was not necessarily what was going to make him successful moving forward. He made it a point to think about how he could continue to prove to others that he was more than just an over-achieving sales guy. Along the way, Ron also learned some very valuable lessons about the importance of focusing not only on the long term for work, but also the long term for his family. While the feedback and resulting challenges were grounded in his work life, Ron was able to draw many parallels in terms of how to make his whole life more effective.

Chapter 4

The Energizer
Making Ideas Contagious

Are you an Energizer type? Start by taking a few minutes to complete the following brief symptom questionnaire.

Please read each of the following statements. Using the scale provided, rate the extent to which each symptom describes you. Total your score by adding up your ratings on individual items. Determine the extent to which this leadership style is reflective of your tendencies based on the final scoring provided.

Rating Scale

1 = This statement hardly describe me
2 = This statement somewhat describes me
3 = This statement definitely describes me

	Please indicate the extent to which each statement describes you.	Little Extent	Some Extent	Great Extent
1.	I feel bored by things like project plans, details, and implementation	1	2	3
2.	I prefer to think about future opportunities rather than current issues	1	2	3
3.	I think that frequent risk taking is essential to job satisfaction	1	2	3

4.	I believe good ideas are worth pursuing, even when they seem impossible	1	2	3
5.	I like to shock people with my bold ideas	1	2	3
6.	I try to inspire and motivate during my presentations	1	2	3
	Total Score			

Total Score	Description
16–18	This is very likely your leadership type
12–15	This may be your leadership type, but you likely demonstrate other types as well
6–11	This is not likely your leadership type

Scott's Story

Scott has had a very successful career in his industry for more than twenty years. He has thoroughly enjoyed each and every experience, having worked in a number of companies during that time. Most recently, when the company he was working for in Pennsylvania merged with another firm in northern California, he found himself on the job market. They offered him the chance to relocate, but this was not something he was open to doing based on his family circumstances. It was all fine and good though, as Scott was used to making these transitions and in fact was enthusiastic about starting fresh. While he would miss the people he had come to know, he felt confident that he would find a whole new set of great colleagues ahead. In his last week with the firm, Scott's confidence about future opportunities was further strengthened based on the unsolicited feedback he received from his boss and others with whom he had worked closely. They spoke about his rare gift of being able to energize and galvanize large groups of people—even folks who did not know him personally. They talked about how much they would miss his natural charisma and uncanny ability to convince senior management to make some pretty bold moves to expand and grow the organization, even in tough times. They joked about how it was almost impossible to pin him down about details or tactics, and he brushed it off by saying that somehow it all worked out and amazing things happened regardless. When he reflected upon his experience with the firm, Scott realized that five years seemed to be about the time at which he got the itch to move on anyway, so maybe this was all a blessing in disguise.

After a few months, Scott was excited to accept a position as Vice President of Operations at a medical supply company. The company was a bit smaller than other places he had been, but in his mind it created a unique opportunity to make his mark. The company was planning to expand the business internationally, and Scott had a number of big ideas about how he could help them make it happen. He spent the first 30 days interviewing all of the senior people in the organization to better understand their business and their thoughts on the possibilities and opportunities related to international expansion, and he put together a comprehensive plan based on his interview findings. At a meeting with all of the senior team present, Scott shared his plan. He had a number of bold ideas about strategies in the international market, including a radical overhaul of the firm's approach to distribution. His charismatic style and dynamic personality helped to get everyone on board and committed to pursuing a number of his ideas. Scott proceeded to assemble a number of taskforces made up of a cross section of senior people to further strategize and devise action plans for moving forward. Scott met with each of the groups to set them on the right path, and to motivate them about the possibilities and what success would afford them all in the years to come.

Scott was the first person in a long time who brought some new and fresh ideas to a company that had historically been known as conservative and staid in its way of doing business. The competition was at their heels in the U.S. and everyone was feeling the pressure to grow market share. The CEO saw proactive international expansion as a perfect remedy, given that the market was nearly untapped for their particular product mix. It was clear that a lot was riding on the impact that Scott could make. The decision was made to establish a strategic partnership with a German organization—a company that was well positioned to help both manufacture and distribute the product within most of Europe. Scott made several trips overseas to get things started, and in fact got a few key people from the U.S. to relocate overseas to help in the process. They were thrilled with the new opportunity and the mood was quite positive from the get go.

A few months into the planning stages, Scott was invited to get involved in some additional discussions to help another division of the company think about how they could expand in the international market. While this was not technically part of his role at the time, Scott was excited by the freshness of it all and got actively engaged and immersed with the senior team to help do for them what he had begun for his own division. His boss, the Division President, was confident that

Scott had the potential to handle both his day job and this other effort on more of a consulting/advisory basis, so he was open to sharing Scott as a resource. Besides, he knew that Scott actually came from a much larger role at his previous company, so he felt like this temporary "consulting" role would be motivating—not to mention getting the attention of the ultimate boss, the CEO of the entire company.

Scott had regular meetings with his boss to keep him updated on things, and each time he brought a new idea. The boss commented about how thrilled they were to have his fresh perspective, and specifically commented that many people had come unsolicited to share their enthusiasm for what Scott brought to the table. While his staff often commented that they wanted to see more of him, they seemed at the same time excited about working for someone who did not micromanage like his predecessor. Everything was good in Scott's world and a part of him enjoyed the feeling of being a rock star in his new organization.

Understanding the Style

We appreciate Energizers like Scott for their passion, conviction, and natural charisma. As an Energizer, you are known to have big, bold, creative ideas about what is possible to achieve, and an almost mesmerizing way of galvanizing others to action. You have a strong personal presence and verge on being "famous" inside and outside of your organization. Your style can be almost seductive by nature, drawing people in to believe in things they might never have thought were possible. You are willing to take risks that others aren't—in presenting ideas and recommendations that will help advance the organization's agenda—and you don't worry much about whether the idea is realistic or practical to implement. For you, the excitement comes from the intellectual and emotional stimulation associated with the ideas themselves, coupled with their ability to rally others around them. Organizations love Energizers because such passion and energy is hard to develop in those who don't naturally have it. You help others think big and explore the unknown—qualities that are particularly appreciated in steady or stagnant environments.

But, like the other styles described in this book, the Energizer too has an Achilles heel. First and foremost, you are typically challenged to maintain the momentum and the energy necessary to see your big ideas through to fruition. Politicians are often Energizers, able to get crowds of people excited and enthusiastic about their ideas, strategies, and potential leadership abilities. Many successful salespeople are Energizers as well, amazingly able to convince customers that they absolutely must have the particular product they are selling. You are uniquely persuasive and convincing about your ideas and why they make sense. Yet, you often lose interest as the idea gets closer to implementation. Your focus on one idea gets quickly replaced by the next big idea that comes along - just like the sales person who is happy to pass the new customer along to the inside service desk once the dotted line has been signed. While Energizers like you have an artful way of building a groundswell of support for their ideas in the beginning—and in an almost mesmerizing way—your followers are sometimes left hanging and wondering where the game plan is and how specifically they are supposed to participate in the plan. The best case is when there is someone in place to carry the torch and pull things through. Worst case, you and your fellow Energizers get the reputation of being "all smoke and mirrors." You may identify a group of people to pull initiatives through, but are not as interested in truly tracking the progress of those efforts to ensure that things are progressing according to plan. Most Energizers abhor details, because in its most fundamental sense, it was the big idea and the chance to get others on board and motivated to believe in something that was at the core of your objective.

Some might argue that aspects of the Energizer style are reminiscent of dating situations that lose their steam. The first date is really exciting and fun and the two people connect in a way that feels authentic and heartfelt. They court for a while and share new and interesting experiences together. She is, unfortunately, disappointed and confused when, after a few great dates, he never calls back. She asks herself, "What just happened? I thought things were going great. I really thought we connected. . . ." He, on the other hand, would simply say that he became bored and restless as soon as the novelty began to fade and the realities of relationship complexities and compromises begin to find their way in to the picture. As an Energizer, you don't want to quickly settle into a routine of going to the movies every Saturday night; you want the excitement and novelty to last. If the other person wants to go to a trendy club, you're more than willing—but not to a family dinner at your mother's house.

Inside organizations, there is often a dilemma when it comes to Energizers in leadership roles. It's easy to appreciate your personal style, because naturally charismatic and motivational people are difficult to come by and even more unrealistic to develop. The organization needs your contagious energy to help galvanize others, particularly when the going gets rough and some positive vibes are needed to turn things around. Your ideas and optimism about the future are cherished. On the flip side though, rarely is there a leadership role in an organization that does not require some level of management to ensure things get done. Things like discipline, process, and structure might make your skin crawl, but without it the ideas and energy are likely to evaporate over time, only to leave unfinished business and disheartened followers.

Watching an Energizer like you "on stage" can be a stimulating, rousing experience. But try to find you later for help running the project they were showcasing and you're often nowhere to be found. You are motivated by being motivational, not by being hands-on. That's great for getting things started, but it can be alienating for a staff that wants their leader to be accessible and available for follow-through.

Your forte is getting others excited and making them believe in the possibilities. You get people enthusiastic and ready to charge ahead. However, when you leave the stage, you don't always leave behind enough information or skill to get the job done. Additionally, when you get people that excited, it can make it difficult for them to prioritize. They can't tell what is important and what is not, and as a result the wrong things may get attention. Motivating people is not all that is needed. There are times when the situation calls for the leader to be composed and thoughtful.

By encouraging people to look at everything through the lens of what is possible, you may not be teaching people to think through all of the consequences of their actions. You need to encourage your people to make sound judgments based on both critical analysis of alternatives and appropriate follow-through so that you and your team collectively can make a lasting impact.

Summary of the Style
Strengths

- Motivates others to do great things
- Is energized by new challenges and unique opportunities
- Demonstrates a strong and impactful presence

Challenges

- Often less effective at implementation and follow-through
- May not always be interested in going deep on issues
- Can be perceived as inauthentic or superficial in relationships
- Needs structure to ensure that the business is truly managed

Prescriptions for This Style

If the story and/or the descriptors of the Energizer resonate with you, consider the following prescriptions as practical tactics and approaches for outsmarting your leadership genes. Review the list in its entirety first, then go back and consider the relevance and appropriateness of each particular item. Make notes in the margins to indicate which of the prescriptions might be worthwhile to incorporate into your plan.

LEADERSHIP PRESCRIPTIONS FOR THE ENERGIZER

Environmental Element	Prescriptions To Consider
Structure	- **Minimize number of direct reports:** You will be most effective operating in a pyramid structure that does not stretch you too thin. Keeping direct reports to a minimum will reduce the potential for frenetic and unfocused activity—and too many new ideas coming into your view. Be selective about which functions or roles are most critical to report directly to you, based on where you believe you personally need to be more closely involved.

Structure (cont'd)	• **Designate a counterpart to mind the store:** Since you may be engaged in diverse activities both inside and outside of the organization, it may make sense to create a role that is responsible for internal business and operations, including day-to-day management of the team. This position can help to establish priorities and discipline around how work gets done, allowing you to focus on exploring new ideas and opportunities. Fill the role with someone who is much more inclined than you are to focus on managing an operation and building discipline into how work is done. The focus needs to be on things such as ensuring accountability, rewarding and recognizing key contributors, and ensuring systems and processes are in place to help develop future talent.
Process	• **Include pragmatists in decision-making activities:** Before coming to an independent conclusion about new ideas or directions, solicit input from others who are practical and realistic by nature. Doing so will not only provide more credibility and boundaries to your ideas, but also help to ensure that the practical implications of things are carefully considered before moving ahead. • **Communicate new ideas with literal business implications:** You may naturally seek to motivate and inspire others with analogies, stories, and the notion of dreams becoming a reality. However, junior level team members need to understand the practical implications of your declarations, and may require a more literal interpretation and message. Your communication should aim to convey ideas with clarity and precision, speaking to things like how the idea will impact others and their roles.

Process (cont'd)	• **Create opportunities to listen:** Since you may often find yourself separated from your team and their daily tasks, it is important to find ways to listen and observe how projects are being pulled through on the ground floor. You may schedule regular staff or town hall type meetings, during which you actively listen rather than introduce new ideas. Use the forum to allow individuals to provide feedback and communicate concerns or issues that they feel need to be addressed in order for them to perform most effectively. Consider having the meetings facilitated by someone who naturally has more discipline and focus as a part of their personality. • **Use documentation as a guide:** Prior to meetings, request (or create) agendas, project plans, outlines, etc. to keep discussions on task. These documents should emphasize tangible business outcomes and execution, rather than the exploration of new ideas. Make a personal commitment to reference the documentation to guide the conversations, even if it may be uncomfortable for you. Be sure to reference previous commitments and accountabilities from earlier meetings so that nothing slips through the cracks. • **Maximize use of administrative tools:** Leverage all the capabilities of things such as calendar reminders, etc. to give you administrative support and ensure that you are reminded of your specific commitments and obligations. Fully leverage such tools for helping you remember such things as staff birthdays, staff anniversaries for years of service, Administrative Professionals Day, etc. so that you will appear to others as thoughtful in ways that are meaningful to them.

Process (cont'd)	• **Meeting management:** Consider incorporating the following prescriptions into how you plan and run your meetings: o Create an agenda and stick to it using a timekeeper—resist adding any new ideas to the agenda. o Prioritize agenda items based on business relevance—not personal interest. o Capture and distribute notes after the meeting to ensure follow-up at the next meeting. o Schedule regular check-in type meetings between larger meetings to ensure important things are kept on track.
People	• **Don't ignore the skeptics:** Two types of people often seduce the Energizer—those who are in awe of their energy and those who are just like them. If you are an Energizer, you may tend to avoid people who are skeptical of their energy and passion. However, such skeptics can force you to examine your big ideas in more depth to identify the ones that will matter most to the organization. These skeptics can also be helpful in ensuring flawless implementation. • **Be sure that others know how to access you:** Your active and wide-ranging work activities might leave your home team feeling neglected. Rather than relying on major events to establish visibility, keep in touch with your staff through simple gestures such as returning emails promptly, making your schedule available, or planning meetings far in advance to ensure that adequate time is blocked out and others can make themselves available. Make a personal commitment to avoid constantly rescheduling such time with staff when something more interesting comes along. Let people know when during the day or evening it is best to reach you, even considering the concept of standard and regular "office hours" such as is typical in an academic environment. The idea is to offer some level of predictability so that people have a regular opportunity to access you as the leader.

People (cont'd)	• **Get a speech writer**: Consider getting the support of a speech writer who will build in substance to back up your motivational ideas. This person will do research and flesh out the details so that others who hear your presentation will get more than just a top line motivational message. Ensure there is an appropriate level of detail built into your presentations to clarify "what's next?"
Culture	In addition to the norms that are naturally aligned with the Energizer's strengths, you should also consider emphasizing the following set of norms within your team: • **Discipline:** Ensure that there is consistency and structure to how work gets done, and that things are seen to completion. • **Accountability:** Use your assistant and your calendar to track the status of projects, and assign individuals/ groups to specific deliverables. Make it clear through your actions that there are consequences for lack of pull-through. • **Focus:** Limit the number of new projects and initiatives that are being introduced at any one time, to enable your staff to prioritize and execute existing work and priorities.

Scott's Story Continued

It is now several months later and the competitive landscape has been fierce for Scott's company, particularly the medical supply division of which he is a part. This has put huge pressure on the situation and everyone is looking much more closely at everything. Scott continues to feel like he is running 90 miles a minute. He has been on a road show to the organization about all of the strategic initiatives that are under way, and about how much new business is possible when everything gets to be fully functioning. He quotes aggressive projections and paints a very positive picture about the future—despite rising concerns that the competition has an edge. He finds it hard to stay connected with all of the various groups and teams he has put in place to think through all the specific steps that need to happen, but in the end reminds himself that these are perfectly capable and competent people who know what they are doing and should be left alone.

One morning Scott is informed that his boss, the Division President, will "no longer be with the organization" after the end of the month, and that a new person is being brought in from the outside. In preparation for the first meeting, the new person asks Scott to come prepared to discuss the key initiatives and to share comprehensive plans with timelines, etc. so that he can get a handle on things. While details are not his strength, Scott scrambles to pull together a few conference calls with the various groups, and to gather materials together for the meeting. Underneath his smooth and charismatic exterior, Scott begins to feel anxious and uncertain. He and the old boss had really hit it off and they had similar styles.

This new guy was definitely cut from a different cloth. In the back of his mind, though, Scott knew he had no other choice but to make the best of things since he was certainly in no position to switch jobs or organizations again. After a tough first meeting, it became apparent there was a new sheriff in town. Scott did a lot of thinking about how he was going to thrive working for someone whom he saw as a micromanager who cared more about silly details than about whether Scott's strategy was the right one to follow. Like it or not, Scott had to figure out a way to make this work.

At the same time as all of this was happening, Scott had a meet-and-greet type lunch with a young ambitious guy named Jeff who had been working in the U.S. sales organization but wanted to get more international exposure. Jeff simply wanted to network and get to know Scott and get some advice. After the first meeting though, Scott got to thinking about how Jeff could actually be of help to him in his situation. Although a bit reluctant at first, Scott decided to offer Jeff a chance to work full-time for six months in support of all of the various international expansion initiatives.

For the next half-year Jeff worked as Scott's right-hand person. He prepared a comprehensive calendar outlining the status of all of the various initiatives, worked closely with each of the teams to ensure that their efforts and progress were tracked, and prepared a bi-weekly packet of materials for Scott to share with his new boss in their one-on-one meetings. He wrote executive summaries each month to give Scott appropriate updates, and kept him abreast of challenges the teams were facing that required his attention, guidance, and expertise. While the level of detail in the documents and the tactical details in the conversations with Jeff drove him crazy, Scott came to appreciate Jeff's ability to keep him out of trouble and focused on the things that mattered to the new boss. Scott still enjoyed the thrill of bringing new ideas to the table, but he came to realize that people like Jeff play a key role in keeping things real. Jeff and Scott developed a solid relationship. Jeff made sure that Scott did not let his energy and thirst for the next big idea trump his commitment to effectively finishing what he had started. Jeff naturally evolved into playing the devil's advocate and being the realist when it came to key decisions about what would and would not work given organizational resources and constraints. Over time, the two became very close colleagues who drove one another crazy at times but also grew to truly appreciate one another's gifts.

Wisdom for Energizers

Energizers' bosses often bring in outside coaches to help the Energizers understand and appreciate the need for follow-through. The biggest concern these bosses raise is that they need to be confident that their Energizers can, in fact, pull something really big and complex through in the organization. While Energizers are beloved for coming up with amazing ideas and galvanizing others around them, most senior leaders, especially in today's business climate, need to concern themselves with bottom line oriented behaviors in their managers. When they are sitting around the table engaged in talent type discussions, they need and want hard and fast evidence that Energizers can deliver on their big ideas.

If you are an Energizer who is interviewing for a new job for example, be sure to focus your conversations on things like how you have been able to turn around a troubled part of an organization, or where you were instrumental in leading a team to implement an entirely new program or way of doing business.

As a leader, you are likely to be faced with unique challenges and dynamics in navigating your way through classic leadership responsibilities and particular leadership events. Like many things in life, if you are insightful about how you typically respond to certain situations, you are in a much better position to self-manage in a way that will allow you to be most effective. What follows is specific advice for Energizers for the following situations:

1. *Making an Impact as a Leader*
2. *Managing and Developing Others*
3. *Relationship Building*
4. *Getting Promoted*
5. *Moving On from the Organization*

Making an Impact as an Energizer

Making an impact is about getting yourself and your work noticed in the organization. It is about developing a positive reputation in the minds of others as someone who has the wherewithal to make things happen and improve the organization and its people in some way. Energizers are often challenged in particular ways in this area.

Being impactful is the Energizer's sweet spot in many ways. However, senior leaders and other thoughtful people in the organization will not be persuaded by your enthusiasm and ideas alone. If you don't have what it takes to set your ideas in motion, you will be seen as superficial and, worst case, an "empty suit." While not necessarily the truth, this is not an attractive description. However, if you don't develop the part of you that can get things done, you will not reach your true leadership potential. Always make sure that you think things through realistically and stick to your ideas. When you get excited in the moment, you can lead others off on a tangent and lose your focus—and focus is a key to maintaining your impact as a leader.

Managing Others as an Energizer

A key element of any leadership role is that of managing and developing talent, and each style is challenged by different aspects of this area of responsibility.

Energizers don't often make the time for managing and developing others. It's not that you don't see the need for development, it's just that you think that you can motivate people to manage their own development. Actually, that's not a bad idea. Most high performers will, in fact, figure out how to develop themselves. However, weaker performers may not. As challenging as it may seem, developing others can truly help you to build a groundswell of support that can multiply your results exponentially.

As an Energizer, you likely have a need to be admired by those you lead. In fact, you may be motivated to spend time developing others in an effort to have them become one of your greatest admirers. People with your personality type actually depend, in some ways, on admirers in order to feel effective in their role. In large part, the admiration of others is a core energy source for you, and actually fuels your desire and interest to keep things progressing, even under challenging circumstances. The other good news is that when you spend time developing those you lead, you also influence them by getting them to believe in why your ideas about their career growth make sense. However, you tend to want to influence individuals not only about their jobs, but also about their beliefs and value systems. If you are a true Energizer, you may have a tendency to view this deeper level of influence as more important (and interesting) than helping those you lead get the skills they need to do the work and get results. Developmentally, it is important to keep in mind that when you are managing people in an organizational context, you need to ensure sufficient focus on influencing them about the results, not just what they believe in or how they view the future.

Building Relationships as an Energizer

Building and maintaining productive working relationships is a key ingredient for the success of every leader and manager. Technical expertise and smarts are in many ways a foregone conclusion. Here is some perspective about the typical dynamics Energizers face in developing effective relationships, and some practical advice and guidance to help things along where needed.

People often perceive Energizers as being superficial. That's because you're usually so interested in and passionate about your plans and ideas that you block out the world around you, and potentially even the people in it. Building authentic and deep relationships is, however, essential to your long-term success. Be straight with people. If you are not really interested in building a relationship with a colleague, don't pretend that you are—but don't shut that person out completely, either. Try to find a happy medium. If you feign more interest or behave more charmingly than the situation requires, others may end up viewing you as shallow and disingenuous. Be as authentic with people as you can, and they will ultimately respect you for it. This may mean delivering difficult messages at times, or tempering your enthusiasm with organizational realities and hard facts.

As an Energizer, you often instantly create what appear to be really intimate attachments—but that's different than true, deep, and lasting relationships. Instant rapport is not the same as a truly meaningful relationship. Often, relationships with Energizers are lopsided—people feel more connected to you than you may feel with them. People attach to you, but you don't necessarily return the attachment. They get the illusion of authenticity based on your charm and charisma. You may not mean to mislead them - but you're ready to move on to the next situation or relationship.

Without meaning to, you may leave people feeling gypped after you've gone, even though you had the best of intentions. Think of Harold Hill, the "Music Man" who would swoop into a town, convince the townsfolk they absolutely needed a marching band, and then abscond with all their hard-earned money. This is not to say that you are conning your peers; this is simply an extreme example of how an Energizer typically works. They charm you hard and fast, and then can quickly move on to the next hot topic or issue.

Often, relationships with Energizers are lopsided—people feel more connected to you than you may feel with them. They get the illusion of authenticity based on your charm and charisma. You may not mean to mislead them, it's just that you're ready to move on to the next situation or relationship.

Additionally, you may want to think about the environment in which you aim to build and nurture relationships. While large group situations may be a comfortable setting for you, authentic and deep relationships require a level of personal intimacy and this is usually established much better in smaller settings and one-on-one. For those people with whom you want to build a relationship, consider things like going to lunch or meeting for a drink or dinner in the evening. You need to ensure that you follow up your initial enthusiasm with more intimate opportunities to learn about others and to allow them to learn more about you.

Getting Promoted as an Energizer

Each style has a unique set of dynamics when it comes to trying to get promoted and dealing with the realities of not having received the promotion they thought they were deserving of. Here are a few pointers for Energizers.

Energizers are always looking for the next great opportunity—so much so that they often neglect their current responsibilities. Stay focused on your current position, understanding that it provides critical opportunities for others to see you as someone who has the capability to operate at a more senior level. Don't ignore or undervalue your present responsibilities—make sure that when you leave a department or organization, it is functioning well.

If you find that you are overlooked for promotions, you may be surprised by the person who actually gets the job. It's probably someone who appears to you to be boring and uninspiring. It may help you to remember that managing and leading requires that a certain level of attention be paid to things such as organization, structure, planning, rules, and consistency—factors that you may feel get in the way of demonstrating your best qualities. By taking the time to master some degree of these skills (and surrounding yourself with others who more naturally bring such strengths), you will possess a hard-to-beat combination of the ability to motivate and galvanize people while also organizing and guiding them to do extraordinary things.

Moving on as an Energizer

At some point or another in your leadership career, you may find yourself having to move on from an organization. If so, you might find the following insights and advice meaningful to ensure that you are able to keep things in a healthy perspective.

If you're an Energizer, you tend to think big. You are optimistic by nature and believe that if you can't inspire people in one environment, then you can in another. However, you can be in such a hurry for immediate success that you don't give others the time to understand or trust you. The key is not to jump ship too soon if you get anxious that the organization is either not accepting of or slow to adopt your way of thinking. It takes people a while to grasp big ideas.

As an Energizer, it is easy for you to get people worked up. They are inspired by your ideas and often feel deeply connected to you as a leader. Then, when something better (in your opinion) comes along, you may leave them behind and (in their minds) leave them hanging. As you travel through your career, remember that it's a small world and you never know when or where you might meet these people again, or need their help in your new position. If you do move on, think about promises you may have made and connections you may want to keep. You want people to think you are a person of your word.

If you are confident that you have been as patient as you can be at allowing the organization enough time to absorb your ideas and they have still not fully embraced them, you may need to ask yourself whether it's because of a key group of people you need to influence (suggesting that perhaps you just need to work in a different part of the organization), or if it's the broader organizational culture that is not responding to your style. Some companies value things like steady execution of sound ideas and are not risk-oriented. If that's the case, there might be an organizational mismatch, and moving on may be just what is needed.

Scott's Story Continued

Fast forward one year. Scott has been getting great feedback from his new boss and he continues to feel engaged in the work. A few of the critical initiatives that were part of the international expansion have been completed, and the financials indicate a noticeable uptick in revenue across the globe. A few of the smaller initiatives that got off the ground in the beginning were curtailed since they were draining resources from more critical efforts. While Scott was disappointed to have to let go of some of his creative ideas, he also recognized that the focus and pull-through in other areas have made all the difference in the end. Jeff, the eager Chief of Staff, grew into his role quite nicely and ultimately became indispensable to Scott. Having worked so closely through such a challenging time brought them close as colleagues, and Jeff came to learn and grow significantly as a professional by being exposed to Scott's visionary ideas and galvanizing style. While Jeff was originally scheduled to rotate to a new position after six months, the decision was made for him to stay an additional year to see through the implementation of all that had been put into motion. Over dinner and drinks during a business trip to Europe, Jeff thanked Scott for all of the exposure and visibility he got in this position—knowing that it would likely put his whole career on the fast track. Scott in turn spoke about how grateful he was to have such an exceptional colleague who he knew certainly made a hugely meaningful difference for him and his career.

Chapter 5

The Guardian
People First

A re you a Guardian type? Start by taking a few minutes to complete the following brief symptom questionnaire.

Please read each of the following statements. Using the scale provided, rate the extent to which each symptom describes you. Total your score by adding up your ratings on individual items. Determine the extent to which this leadership style is reflective of your tendencies based on the final scoring provided.

Rating Scale

1 = This statement hardly describe me
2 = This statement somewhat describes me
3 = This statement definitely describes me

	Please indicate the extent to which each statement describes you.	Little Extent	Some Extent	Great Extent
1.	I feel that it's very important to create a nurturing work environment	1	2	3
2.	I prefer for my team to operate like a family	1	2	3
3.	I think it is important to know people very well to work effectively together	1	2	3

4.	I feel ambivalent about delivering difficult feedback, because I worry that the recipient will take the criticism personally	1	2	3
5.	I believe that a manager should protect their team from the crossfire	1	2	3
6.	I believe that it's a boss's responsibility to ensure that people feel happy at work	1	2	3
	Total Score			

Total Score	Description
16–18	This is very likely your leadership type
12–15	This may be your leadership type, but you likely demonstrate other types as well
6–11	This is not likely your leadership type

Gerry's Story

Gerry is a Director of Human Resources in a large food service company. He has been with the company for over 15 years, rising through the ranks from a customer service position. He has long-standing relationships with several people in the organization, many of whom have been working there since the organization grew from a mom and pop shop to a major player in its industry. Gerry is well liked and has received a number of company awards over the years, even though he didn't always get along perfectly with Sharon, the CEO.

Gerry is entrenched in the lives of others. He knows all about the personal lives of his direct reports, knows who eats lunch with whom, which staffers are buddy-buddy, and even which of them don't like each other. He is engaging and warm and makes everyone he meets feel welcome.

However, things have been particularly challenging for Gerry this year. It seemed to him that Sharon was even less accessible than usual, and a lot more "all business."

Despite their differences, Sharon asked Gerry to help her form a new task force which would address an important issue. The company was experiencing unexpected competitor activity and was losing money fast. Sharon asked Gerry to help her identify who should be on this strategic internal team. One of the people he proposed was Dan, the head of the Customer Relations department. Gerry had known Dan for years and they had a very close relationship. Their families often socialized together, including multiple weekend trips to Gerry's beach house on the Chesapeake. Gerry knew that Dan wanted to get promoted, and saw this as a way for him to get needed exposure to senior people. Gerry discussed the idea of the task force with Dan when they went out to dinner that week, although he swore Dan to secrecy since the final taskforce members had not been officially announced.

When Gerry met with Sharon to finalize her recommendations, she vetoed a number of the players Gerry suggested, including Dan. Gerry was stunned, but knew he had no other choice but to go back and explain the situation to Dan. He avoided Dan for a week, and after several sleepless nights, finally told him what had transpired. While they were longstanding friends and colleagues, Dan gave Gerry an earful because of what he perceived as false promises; he felt that Gerry had not tried hard enough to convince Sharon that he could be a key player on the team. The two did not speak for a few weeks after that. Gerry felt a great deal of inner turmoil, but was unclear about what he could have done differently. His only way of processing through his feelings was to talk about the situation to others he could trust. His wife listened for a while, but after some time she told Gerry that he had become unreasonably obsessed with this and he had to stop. He took what she said to heart, but privately played the situation over and over again in his head. He soon came to realize that this situation was all too familiar—especially in the last few years since he had become a much more senior leader in the organization. The relationships he had built were the bedrock of his success and allowed him to get a lot of things done. However, he realized that in this instance his good intentions backfired in a pretty unattractive way. What would this mean for his relationship with Dan? Should he go back to Sharon and push harder to get Dan included? What would this do to his own reputation?

Understanding the Style

Guardians are those who focus on relationships and work hard to make sure that they are harmonious and positive. As a Guardian, you deliver results for the organization, but are best known for your ability to develop and nurture long-lasting relationships with others. This unique focus on relationships in the workplace makes you fun to work with because you aim to create a social type setting where people can get to know one another as people, not just work colleagues. You're the type of the person who spends time getting everyone in the office to chip in for the receptionist's engagement gift. Or the one who plans regular out-of-office social gatherings to help the team bond. When you leave an organization, you remain in regular touch with former colleagues via email and social networking. On a fundamental level, you pride yourself on your ability and commitment to watch over others and create a "safe place" where they will be out of harm's way. Guardians are especially tuned in to the needs and interests of others. In many ways, it is as though having the relationships, in and of themselves, is what is important to you. These relationships provide fuel for your work efforts. You often have a reputation for protecting those who report to you from the perceived ferociousness and political realities of the larger organization. You might even see yourself as the necessary umbrella during a torrential downpour. Many people who have worked for Guardian types would probably say they enjoyed their experience and felt nurtured and supported. When asked, many would speak to the sense of loyalty and commitment they had to the Guardian as their leader, in exchange for the unspoken protection they received from the challenges often found in the broader organization.

While we love Guardians for all the obvious reasons, they definitely have their challenges, especially the higher up they go in an organization. This is particularly true in broad leadership roles where being able to balance relationships and business is a must—and the impact of not doing so is particularly problematic.

The fundamental issue gets down to your inability to temper your nurturing and supportive side with an ability to truly look at situations objectively—and to address the tough stuff, either people or business related, head on. High performers might specifically notice that you were not able deal with poor performers in a timely way. While they may like you personally, they may doubt your ability to effectively manage the performance of those that report to you.

Unfortunately, the very thing that makes people appreciate you is the same thing that gets you into trouble in leadership roles. Perhaps the biggest challenge of this style is your ineffectiveness at managing relationship boundaries at work. Simply put, your relationship orientation and focus gets in the way of your ability to achieve business results. You are often tempted to let poor performance slip, you don't ensure enough personal accountability, and you frequently avoid conflict with peers in meetings because you want everybody to get along.

The problem is your inability to separate the value of helping and supporting others from the need to make the tough call. Some low performers may take advantage of you by asking for, and getting, special exceptions which annoys higher performers who feel you give in too easily to the wrong kind of people. In the end, any good leader needs to balance the importance of relationships with the need to achieve business outcomes, and when these two things are out of kilter nobody wins. While you work very hard to create a positive atmosphere where your employees feel supported and nurtured, those same employees often feel resentful, angry, and deeply disappointed if you later deliver a difficult message—or worse yet, have to let someone go because of disappointing performance. This is exactly what happened to Dan and why he became so upset with Gerry. While Gerry had good intentions in trying to get Dan exposure on the key project, Dan ultimately felt betrayed when Gerry was unable to pull it through for him. Initially, you make people feel special, but later on this feeling can deteriorate because you can't always keep your promises. Ultimately, the very thing you were trying to do to help others backfires and becomes a problem.

As a Guardian, you're often like a parent who desperately wants to be a friend to your kids. In your quest for connection, you forget that your primary job is to keep the child headed in the right direction and not to be a pal. There are times when it's appropriate to come down hard on a child who is misbehaving or going down the wrong path. The parent/child relationship requires the older (and hopefully wiser) individual to maintain control and set boundaries. The boss/employee relationship carries these same requirements. What your people want is a true boss—not an overly protective parent who does not prepare them for the real world. You may find that you are liked and appreciated by many, but not necessarily viewed as effective in the truest sense of the word.

The depth of the Guardians' relationships also means that they have information about people and situations that they probably should not have. It's not that Guardians pry inappropriately (although some do because they see this as a way of connecting); it's that their personal style may lead others to share information with them that they later can't filter out when it comes to making business decisions. Having this information would not be problematic if the Guardian is able to be discrete in using this information appropriately inside the organization. Ultimately, others can view them as untrustworthy and, in the worst case, unprofessional—neither of which are the Guardian's intent.

Because Guardians tend to focus much of their energy on those to whom they are closest (e.g., direct reports), they often do not put sufficient energy into influencing upwards in the organization and keeping in touch with what is happening from a business perspective. As a result, they are typically not well-known by more senior leadership, and this can ultimately be career limiting. In addition, Guardians run the risk of being uninformed about what is going on in the broader organization, and this can mean that the people below them are at a disadvantage as well. When Guardians don't take the time to get involved or influence those above them, the efforts and talents of the entire group may go unnoticed.

Summary of the Style
Strengths

- Highly attuned to people and cares about their needs and interests
- Delivers well against pre-defined goals
- Tends to have deep, lasting relationships with others
- Works hard to engender loyalty and commitment of others

Challenges

- Overly focused on creating and maintaining harmony
- Can be reluctant to take on tough issues and/or deliver difficult messages
- Focuses more attention on the short term than the long term
- Often better at managing down than managing up in the organization

Prescriptions for Guardians

If the story and/or the descriptors of the Guardian resonate with you, consider the following prescriptions as practical tactics and approaches for outsmarting your leadership genes. Review the list in its entirety first, then go back and consider the relevance and appropriateness of each particular item. Make notes in the margins to indicate which of the prescriptions might be worthwhile to incorporate into your plan.

LEADERSHIP PRESCRIPTIONS FOR THE GUARDIAN

Environmental Element	Prescriptions To Consider
Structure	• **Develop a small advisory council of peers to help you better manage difficult performance-related situations:** Identify a key group of peers who can help be your conscience when you struggle with difficult performance-related issues for your direct reports. Seek their advice and counsel around how to make sure you are clearly focused on delivering a crisp and concise message regarding performance gaps, regardless of your personal feelings. Choose people for this peer group who are not Guardians by nature, but instead more critical and business oriented.
	• **Minimize the number of your direct reports:** Since your natural orientation is to take care of people, try to limit the number of direct reports you have so that you have fewer people to attend to on a day-to-day basis. This will help to ensure that you don't get distracted by an overabundance of small talk, and that you limit the number of opportunities to go too deep in relationship building, with potential to mismanage boundaries.

Structure (cont'd)	• **Make sure you have a person who can work as a buffer between you and those who report to you:** This individual will operate as your "second in command" and be focused on ensuring that accountability is infused in the culture and results are achieved in a timely manner. This person could serve as the first point of contact if issues arise around completing work. In this manner, you will be able to create better boundaries between you and those who report directly to you, ensuring that personal relationships don't interfere with driving toward outcomes. Think carefully about the type of personality you bring into such a role, so that it truly serves the purpose you need.
Process	• **Rely on clearly defined criteria to help you manage and reward performance:** As you work to develop and motivate those you lead to improve their performance, you will need to be clear about what you are measuring. Communicate clearly that rewards will come based on achieved outcomes and demonstrated competencies. Communication of the criteria in advance will help alleviate the tendency you may have to allow your personal feelings to interfere with using sound, objective judgment in evaluating performance or providing rewards. • **Develop a systematic way to assess the talent of your team:** A methodical, objective review will help you fully understand the skills and talents inherent in your current staff, and how you can leverage them to achieve greater business results. Leverage available internal resources such as talent management experts within Human Resources to help you design and implement a process that is fair and consistent. This will ensure that you are seeing your team's capabilities objectively against some pre-defined criteria, instead of relying on personal relationships and feelings about others.

Process
(cont'd)
	• **Get support from your boss for critical and difficult decisions:** Seek support for critical decisions you need to make. While you will still be responsible for the decision and its communication, your boss's support can help to give you the courage to deliver the message without feeling like you are going it alone. Talking with your boss will help you gain more perspective about the issue(s) and reduce any personal guilt or discomfort you may experience when making tough decisions or giving difficult performance feedback.
	
	• **Manage delivery of difficult messages by being fully prepared:** When you have to communicate a key message that may be opposed by others, prepare yourself by writing it down first. For example, you will be more likely to deliver all of the key messages during a difficult performance feedback session if you have prepared it beforehand and can refer to a written document that contains the points you want to make.
	
	• **Meeting management:** Consider incorporating the following prescriptions into how you plan and run your meetings:
	
	  o Disrupt consensus by taking a vote on issues.
	
	  o Document your point of view before the meeting to avoid equivocating when the meeting is in session.
	
	  o Record and distribute meeting notes to enforce accountability.
	
	  o Differentiate between outstanding individual performance (selectively) by creating an accolade to highlight extraordinary contributions.

People	• **Select results-oriented people for your staff**: If you need to fill a key position in your area of responsibility, focus clearly on candidates who can help balance out your Guardian style. Consider candidates who are definitively results oriented, for example. These types of individuals will help you stay focused on outcomes. • **Involve a broad group in selection:** Intentionally include business-minded people in the process of selection, so that you do not get seduced by how much you may personally like a candidate. • **Manage others based on final outcomes, not incremental progress:** Be mindful of your tendency to stay overly involved and to manage specific tasks and progress. Instead, keep your focus on final outcomes. What you may think is moral support may be perceived by your team as too much oversight and involvement for things they feel like they can handle independently—especially the very talented staff. Over time, your constant support may become a crutch for some employees and limit their development as independent thinking professionals. Without meaning to, your team will miss opportunities to stretch themselves by tackling issues on their own and learning from their mistakes.
Culture	In addition to the norms that are naturally aligned with the Guardian's strengths, you should also consider emphasizing the following set of norms within your team: • **Constructive conflict:** Encourage others to offer their points of view or to play devil's advocate. Create a safe space to disagree so that all points of view can be considered before final decisions are made. To make it real, assign someone the role of playing devil's advocate at meetings. Have this role be a rotating responsibility so everyone gets practice and over time it becomes a more natural way to operate.

Culture (cont'd)	<ul><li>**Efficiency and discipline**: Set an example of efficiency and discipline by the way that you handle your time and the expectations you have of others in this regard. Start your meetings promptly and follow the agenda you prepare. Be on time for the meetings to which you are invited and limit small talk for the sake of getting to the business at hand.</li><li>**Clear accountability**: Have clearly documented goals and objectives for all the major initiatives within your area of responsibility, and a means for tracking the progress of those on your staff who have accountability for helping you achieve your goals.</li><li>**Boundary management**: Establish to those around you that managing boundaries between work and personal relationships is a cornerstone of how you believe you can be successful together. This is not something that is typically communicated, but doing so overtly can help your staff understand what is expected and as a result not misinterpret your behavior. This is important at the beginning of relationships, before things get too far down the road.</li></ul>

Gerry's Story Continued

Gerry was anxious when he got his next performance review from Sharon, the CEO. He was stunned when Sharon gave him very direct feedback, saying that she did not feel that she was getting what she needed from him, and that she was disappointed with how little the department had accomplished in the past year relative to her expectations. She indicated in no uncertain terms that the word around the organization was that he lacked credibility and did not use the level of discretion she would expect from a person in the most senior HR role. She was clear that she wanted to see Gerry improve in his ability to "make the tough calls" and not let his history or relationships with others get in the way. She indicated that until she saw Gerry's behavior noticeably change, she simply was not comfortable putting him on her newly-formed, hand-selected executive committee which was made up of several of Gerry's long time peers.

When Gerry found the guts to ask for her specific examples, Sharon cited (among many examples) the fact that he did not effectively handle the situation with Dan and the strategic task force. She had heard through others that he had essentially promised Dan a spot on the team, when, in fact, it was not his call to make. Gerry was devastated—as though all of his hard work, dedication, and strong relationships in the organization were meaningless. He wondered whether it was time to look for a job elsewhere if this is what his boss thought of him.

Gerry had a number of close friends outside of work and decided to consult one of them, Bob, about his situation. As it turned out, Bob had been in a similar situation in his old job and thought that perhaps the same advice he was given would be helpful to Gerry. Bob suggested that Gerry demonstrate more discipline and information sharing when contributing to critical decisions he had to make on his job, instead of going it alone and just relying on his experience and instinct. Specifically, he suggested that Gerry form a small team of trusted colleagues for important decisions. This group of close colleagues, if well selected, could be helpful in ensuring that Gerry's personal feelings about people did not interfere with sound business decisions. Gerry was initially resistant to the idea because he thought that it would make him look less competent and unable to handle things on his own, especially after all his years of experience. Bob was eventually able to convince him to give it a try for six months and let the results speak for themselves. Knowing that Bob had nothing but the best intentions, Gerry decided it was worth a shot.

Gerry identified a small, cross-functional advisory group of four people whose role was to advise him and to strategize about how to address HR issues that came out of Sharon's executive committee. In selecting the team, he was careful to heed Bob's very clear counsel not to just pick his favorites, but to assemble a team that could offer sound, objective, logical advice.

Additionally, after he got over the sting of his conversation with Sharon, Gerry realized that he had invested too much into the company to just pack his bags and move on. He decided to make a bold move to help Sharon see that he was committed to doing whatever it would take. When the situation presented itself, Gerry asked Sharon if one of the key openings in his group could be replaced with a high-potential person from the business—instead of an HR person. He explained that he felt it was necessary for him and his group to get more in touch with what it takes to run the business successfully—by getting more of a line perspective instead of a staff perspective. Sharon was delighted with the idea and immediately gave Gerry a few recommendations about individuals who might be appropriate for the position. Things were looking up.

Wisdom for Guardians

From a career perspective, you need to be particularly focused on finding an organization where your natural affinity for people will be appreciated and supported. This is not to say that you can't be successful in any type of organization. However, our experiences show that the more that you are aligned with the values, norms, and philosophies of the broader organization, the more satisfaction you will find. While more straight-laced, formal types of organizations are probably fine for the Olympians of the world, the quarterly pressure to perform in order to meet expectations often makes Guardians feel disingenuous or unable to be true to themselves. If you are in job-search mode, you should pay particularly close attention to the signs and symbols unveiled to you in your current role—and to proactively ask questions and listen intently to what you learn. In this way, you can assess for yourself whether your more nurturing ways will be truly embraced in the organization you are considering.

As a leader, you are likely to be faced with unique challenges and dynamics in navigating your way through classic leadership responsibilities and particular leadership events. Like many things in life, if you are insightful about how you typically respond to certain situations, you are in a much better position to self-manage in a way that will allow you to be most effective. What follows is specific advice for Guardians for the following situations:

1. *Making an Impact as a Leader*
2. *Managing and Developing Others*
3. *Relationship Building*
4. *Getting Promoted*
5. *Moving On from the Organization*

Making an Impact as a Guardian

Making an impact is about getting yourself and your work noticed in the organization. It is about developing a positive reputation in the minds of others as someone who has the wherewithal to make things happen and improve the organization and its people in some way. Guardians are often challenged in particular ways in this area.

It's challenging and difficult for you to support everyone in your department while at the same time rewarding stellar performance. To Guardians, people are equal. Yet, to the organization, high performers are clearly valued more than low performers. To combat your Guardian genes, remember that it is more important to be respected as a leader than to be liked. Similarly, it is also more important to respect others than to like them in a work setting. You can show everyone respect—even those with whom you do not have a strong relationship. When high and low performers see that you respect them as individuals and that you are going to reward and recognize people based on actual performance and contribution, they will respect you as a leader and you will be able to be more impactful in the organization.

As a Guardian, you usually have the best of intentions. You want harmony and tranquility above all else, and really aim to help others. Remember though, being liked by others does not always help them in the end. There are certain things you have to do if you're truly interested in helping people and want to manage and lead them effectively. Sometimes you may have to be unpopular or unfair, deliver a difficult message, or be firm when you'd rather be friendly. While this may make you feel awkward or uncomfortable, in the end you will actually be helping the other person get something they really want (e.g., the feedback they need so they can improve and get promoted). The downside may be the challenge of dealing with your own feelings, but the upside is what is likely to come of your new behavior. You have to take the long view on this one, and trust that each time you demonstrate courage to say what needs to be said, it becomes easier and more rewarding. Keep focused on the bigger purpose and greater good, even if it does not feel great on a micro level. In practical terms, it may help people to understand the bigger picture if you take the time to explain why you did what you did to help them.

Managing Others as a Guardian

A key element of any leadership role is that of managing and developing talent, and each style is challenged by different aspects of this area of responsibility.

Taking care of and knowing about others is different than managing and developing them. For example, spending time getting to know your employees and certain aspects of their personal lives can be beneficial. Learning things like people's hobbies, favorite restaurants or travel destinations, and their children's interests can be relevant and helpful as you try to build personal connections. However, it is ultimately far more important to make an accurate and objective assessment of what your employees need developmentally and how they learn best. Do they need fundamental training or just additional time and seasoning to perform more effectively? Do they learn best by reading and applying concepts, or are they the type that simply needs to jump in head first and learn from their mistakes? When you take the time to learn these particular kinds of things about your people, your efforts and developmental approach can be appropriately targeted such that closing the gaps will produce meaningful results.

Additionally, remember that having a satisfying, non-confrontational relationship with your direct reports may be comfortable for you, but it may also make it tough for honesty and authenticity to prevail. For people to truly develop and become better professionals, they need you to be straightforward and honest in your feedback, so that important messages are not shrouded or confusing. You don't want people to feel that they can't say the difficult things because it might hurt someone's feelings or result in uncomfortable interactions. For a group to become truly high performing, it is most important to reward those who can introduce constructive conflict in a situation and remain collegial colleagues afterwards. If you as the leader model this type of behavior, you will be rewarded with long-lasting, mutually respectful relationships.

Building Relationships as a Guardian

Building and maintaining productive working relationships is a key ingredient for the success of every leader and manager. Technical expertise and smarts are in many ways a foregone conclusion. Here is some perspective about the typical dynamics Guardians face in developing effective relationships, and some practical advice and guidance to help things along where needed.

This is your strength and your weakness at the same time. Your problem areas are maintaining boundaries and curtailing the number of intimate relationships you develop at work. If you try to build special relationships with everyone, you can come across as being insincere. It may be to your advantage to develop various types of relationships with your staff, but it is not necessary to be close friends with everyone in order for you or your group to be successful. In the end, you will build stronger relationships if you focus on honesty and balance rather than trying to be everything to everybody.

As a Guardian, you are more likely to build relationships with people who are most like you. However, by doing so you may miss the chance and the value of developing relationships with a broader range of people whose styles may be very different, whose opinions may vary greatly from yours, and who may be a real challenge to you interpersonally. If you don't develop this breadth of relationships, you may find yourself out of the loop or disconnected from what's really going on inside the organization. Again, Guardians tend to develop relationships down the organization rather than up. By way of example, we coach a woman named Ariel. She is in charge of a special projects group within a larger organization. She has a strong bond with the people under her—almost like a mother hen. She takes care of them and tries to do as much as she can for them. However, Ariel hasn't invested any time in the political relationships around her. As a result, she has found herself unaware of several important changes being planned for the company's future—things that will definitely impact her and her group. In that way, she is not helping her people at all.

It is important to remember that in most business situations, it is better to have associates and colleagues than to make true blue friends. You find those kinds of friends outside of the boundaries of work. If not, you are going to find yourself with a moral dilemma every time a sticky situation arises. How will you handle it if you have to fire your best friend? Or if you find out that he or she is being demoted to a lower position (and your boss has sworn you to secrecy)? In order to avoid these situations, you need to put appropriate boundaries around friendships at work.

Getting Promoted as a Guardian

Each style has a unique set of dynamics when it comes to trying to get promoted and dealing with the realities of not having received the promotion they thought they were deserving of. Here are a few pointers for Guardians.

As a Guardian, you probably assume that the organization will automatically acknowledge your contributions; therefore, you need not do anything more than a good job. Underneath it all, you may expect others to take care of you just as you take care of them. However, it is important for you to pay attention to what the organization values in terms of advancement. You must be able to tactfully advocate for yourself and let it be known that you are interested in the job. Don't be surprised, even when you have a great relationship with the boss, when promotions are announced and you are not on the list. Having a strong relationship with the boss does not necessarily mean that you are viewed as promotable. Instead of spending so much time making sure you are liked, focus your time on understanding what is required to be promoted. Being well-liked will not get you on a high-performance team unless you also have strong skills at the next level.

Moving on as a Guardian

At some point or another in your leadership career, you may find yourself having to move on from an organization. If so, you might find the following insights and advice meaningful to ensure that you are able to keep things in a healthy perspective.

It's more difficult for Guardians to move on than for any other type. You tend to value loyalty, commitment, and dedication and you don't want to disrupt the relationships you've worked so hard to form. Once you develop relationships with others or a connection with the organization, you actually don't want to let go. You may even try to talk upper management out of letting you go. You may believe that people are unaware of your true value to the organization. You may also have blinders on when it comes to how decisions are made in the organization. You probably think they are based on relationships when in reality they are made strategically.

Be that as it may, at some point you will probably have to move on. It's important not to create drama as you are transitioning. Also, you should not have to make the organization let you know that it is time to move on...you should read the signs and know that your time has come. Examples of signs include not being invited to key meetings, having seemingly good ideas dismissed out of hand, and not getting selected for unique and forward-thinking projects. It's better if you have some control of the situation so that it will feel like you are leaving on your own terms, not theirs. Keep in mind that moving on does not have to be viewed as a bad thing. You need to reframe it as an opportunity to go to a new situation where you can develop new relationships. For you in particular, the best way to leave is to have a vision or idea of where you are going and the types of people with whom you would like to work. It's easier to let go when you know what's next and feel good about working toward something you truly want.

Guardians often attempt to carry on relationships long after they should have been severed. Once you leave an organization, it's often time to leave those relationships behind and focus on solidifying new ones. Richard, a managing editor in a large publishing firm, was surprised when he was let go, even though many others in the company were being laid off. Three months later he was still calling people at the company, which made them feel uncomfortable. It put them in an awkward position. Richard was trying to keep a foot in the door, but the people still there didn't really want to gossip about office business. This didn't make Richard look good in their eyes, and it actually hurt him in the end. These were people he might have used for networking and references, but who were now less supportive and more reticent to help. Remember that you have only so much mental energy. The more you stay hooked into the energy and the politics of your old job, the less you have available for what's ahead.

Gerry's Story Continued

Fast forward—one year later. Gerry grew a great deal as a leader and was actually excited about the progress he felt he had made. While his contentious relationship with Sharon had thrown him for a loop, Gerry began to realize that her intent was not malicious, and that she was simply doing the job she was asked to do by the Board—turn the place around after profitability had slipped due to economic changes.

As for his personal advisory council, things were functioning quite well. Gerry appreciated the perspective they brought on key issues and it became more obvious to him that there were considerations he was simply missing when he made critical HR decisions on his own (e.g., impact on productivity, impact on bottom line dollars, etc.). The group developed a structure for how often they would get together, and about the kinds of decisions on which they could advise. Gerry learned to maintain appropriate boundaries so that his old habits of going overboard on relationships did not interfere with his ability to do what was objectively the best answer for the organization.

As for Maggie, the person Gerry brought into Human Resources to provide more business perspective, things were a little bumpier. Some members of the HR team (many of whom had been in place as a group for years together) had a hard time accepting Maggie because she was not "one of them." At the same time, Maggie was concerned that the HR experts simply did not have a clue about what kinds of programs and processes would truly be embraced by the business. For the first few months, they did not see Maggie as credible because she had no HR background. Because Gerry knew that he needed this new relationship to work (since he was the one who suggested it to Sharon), he decided to hold a teambuilding session for the HR department. The goal was to keep unspoken feelings and misunderstandings from interfering with all the work that had to be done. Because Gerry realized that his tendency would be to shy away from anything that might be confrontational or hurt someone's feelings, he hired an outside consultant to facilitate the session, knowing that some of the issues might be delicate and require skilled facilitation. The group established new norms for working together, and got their issues and concerns out in the open in a constructive way. After an awkward start, the final feedback was overwhelmingly positive and the group bonded in a way that even went beyond Gerry's expectations. Upon reflection, Gerry came to recognize that while he was not likely to change fundamentally, introducing some basic changes into his environment (e.g., building the small advisory group, hiring a business person into his HR department, and having an outsider facilitate a teambuilding session) could help him to compensate for his weaknesses and allow him to be a more impactful leader and contributor.

Chapter 6

The Guru
Mastery Is Everything

Are you a Guru type? Start by taking a few minutes to complete the following brief symptom questionnaire.

Please read each of the following statements. Using the scale provided, rate the extent to which each symptom describes you. Total your score by adding up your ratings on individual items. Determine the extent to which this leadership style is reflective of your tendencies based on the final scoring provided.

Rating Scale

1 = This statement hardly describe me
2 = This statement somewhat describes me
3 = This statement definitely describes me

	Please indicate the extent to which each statement describes you.	Little Extent	Some Extent	Great Extent
1.	I think it's more important to work with technically competent people than people I get along well with	1	2	3
2.	I believe that any activity that takes me away from focusing on my area of expertise is a waste of my time	1	2	3

3.	I seek to identify the right answer no matter what it takes	1	2	3
4.	I think when goals are clear, smart people should be able to manage themselves without much direct supervision	1	2	3
5.	I like to work on solving complex problems alone	1	2	3
6.	I am the "go to" resource to others for answering challenging questions in my area of expertise	1	2	3
	Total Score			

Total Score	Description
16–18	This is very likely your leadership type
12–15	This may be your leadership type, but you likely demonstrate other types as well
6–11	This is not likely your leadership type

Jolie's Story

Jolie is the head of information technology for a leading mergers and acquisition firm. She possesses a world-class educational pedigree, and was destined from the start to make a major impact on the business community. Jolie is attractive, athletic, and poised, with a quiet self-confidence about her. She graduated from Stanford with a J.D.—M.B.A., and made simultaneously earning a law degree and business degree look easy. Her secret passion is entering (and often) winning national chess competitions. Jolie is almost always the smartest person in the room... so smart that people are happy that she is on their team because, like a hired gun, she almost always gets it right. She's even been featured in several IT and business magazines as an innovative thinker and up-and-coming leader. She is sought after in her area of expertise, and sometimes you get the feeling that the organization gets nervous about how reliant they are on what she knows. At the same time, while the organization appreciates her contributions immensely, they feel conflicted about how well she has been able to transition to being a broader leader with responsibility for others.

Jolie's consistent success landed her the job as head of the department, even though she prefers the technical work of focusing on strategies for predicting the success of a particular merger or acquisition. As the competition for certain mergers heated up, Jolie felt that departmental issues were interfering with her ability to focus on the results she had promised the organization. Instead of addressing these issues head-on, however, she avoided them, like a turtle pulling its head back into its shell. The issues continued to worsen.

Another problem for Jolie was staffing. She realized that she did not have enough trained supervisors to observe, monitor, and manage the performance of others. In addition, the lines of authority were not clear, which caused constant turf battles amongst even her most senior people, whom Jolie felt were well paid and had enough experience to know better. Her boss told her she needed more managerial talent and specifically more women and minorities in her group. While she recognized this as an authentic need for the organization to be its best, she simply did not want to be overly involved or personally accountable to make it happen—this wasn't what she had signed up for! The stress of managing her department ultimately prompted her to give serious thought to quitting and playing chess full-time (and she could afford to do so). However, she was loyal to her company and wanted to try and fix the leadership problem that was created on her watch. While Jolie felt that she would be best utilized as the in-house expert, the organization could not afford that luxury. Jolie needed to become a fully functioning leader.

Understanding the Style

If you're a Guru like Jolie, you probably became a leader because of your sheer intellectual horsepower and ability to solve the most vexing problems. Your knowledge and educational pedigree are superior to that of your peers internally and externally, which ultimately provides a competitive advantage for the organization. As a Guru, you typically have deep and narrow expertise on a particular topic, and are regarded as being the go-to person in your given field. You are completely absorbed by your craft, and are continuously learning in order to remain current with trends and developments. You are motivated by knowing everything that there is to know about your subject matter, and doing so requires a rare combination of focus, passion, and natural ability.

You are likely to view tasks outside of your specific function as wasteful distractions. Why spend a day at an offsite teambuilding retreat or writing performance reviews when you could be discovering a breakthrough solution? You understand that other tasks need to be accomplished; however, in most cases you will procrastinate or delegate those tasks to someone else. You won't be found socializing in the hallways either, or playing office politics. You are dedicated to the work itself, and while acclaim often finds you, recognition is not a primary motivation.

Extreme Gurus almost always lack the skills (and desire) to form deep relationships at work or the vision to carry their organizations into the future. Instead they are firmly entrenched in the work of being best in class.

Gurus are best when working with people who are self-managing. You're not particularly interested or curious about the affairs of your staff, and prefer not to become entangled in "people problems." You believe that high-potential employees should be able to develop themselves, and do not fancy yourself as a coach or mentor. While you may take individual people whom you believe are smart and teach them your craft in an apprentice type fashion, you do not focus on guiding others around the broader issues related to personal effectiveness. Because you believe that success is all the feedback one needs, you will likely try to avoid people who require constant feedback or motivation to keep them energized.

The focus on your discipline enables you to offer deeper and more thoughtful outcomes for the organization. You are likely to generate innovative and unique approaches to business and organizational challenges as you seek to advance within your field. You may even be known as the intellectual superstar within the organization—think of a top surgeon, financial wizard, or celebrated scholar who puts their organization on the map. Your thought leadership provides integrity, superior thinking, and discipline to the organization, and your intellectual clout keep the rest of us from feeling like we are flying by the seat of our pants.

While others truly appreciate the unique and special value you bring to the organization, you face your own unique set of challenges as a leader. People who work for you have a high degree of admiration for you, but may at the same time feel unappreciated and under-motivated. It can be a struggle for you to rally the troops and demonstrate authentic enthusiasm, as you might view this as overly theatrical. It is also not uncommon for you to receive feedback from direct reports indicating management deficiencies stemming from your lack of interest in developing others. You often neglect to consider the aspirations of your staff, and rarely reflect on how others' unique talents and strengths can best be utilized. Your own career development may even be an afterthought, as your persistent focus prevents you from reflecting on how you got to where you are or what you need to do to achieve the next step in your career progression. Because you don't spend time reflecting even for yourself, it is often challenging for you to help others navigate the informal organization for career development purposes. You typically just keep moving projects and work forward, with the underlying assumption that the rest will take care of itself.

Summary of the Style
Strengths

- Expertise offers competitive advantages to the organization
- Learning, research, and knowledge acquisition is valued
- High standards are valued and rewarded

- Employees are allowed to act independently and are managed on results

Challenges

- Focuses more on the work itself, but at the expense of building a motivational climate
- Limited attention paid to organization infrastructure issues such as effective communication and decision-making norms
- Limited focus on motivating and developing others
- Can be insular and lack a broader organizational mindset

Prescriptions for Gurus

If the story and/or the descriptors of the Guru resonate with you, consider the following prescriptions as practical tactics and approaches for outsmarting your leadership genes. Review the list in its entirety first, then go back and consider the relevance and appropriateness of each particular item. Make notes in the margins to indicate which of the prescriptions might be worthwhile to incorporate into your plan.

LEADERSHIP PRESCRIPTIONS FOR THE GURU

Environmental Element	Prescriptions To Consider
Structure	• **Minimize direct reports:** The accountabilities associated with managing a large staff are not compatible with your likely preference for working on tasks that require careful contemplation and technical expertise. Take time to think through which particular roles are most critical as direct reports, based on business need, and the determination of where you should be most closely involved. Having too many direct reports simply sets you up for getting negative feedback from a large group of folks who are frustrated because they don't feel like they get enough access to you as the leader. The fewer the better is the name of the game with direct reports for a Guru. • **Diversify your team.** Avoid organizing solely on the basis of technical expertise. You should blend roles to align with the organization's goals and mission. Additionally, give careful thought to factors such as personality type, ambition level, work style, etc. For example, be careful to ensure that you demonstrate that you value a broad range of characteristics by having both experts and generalist types positioned at equal levels in your structure. Consider involving human resources staff to help ensure that your structure is balanced between experts and non-experts. • **Outsource leadership:** Consider assigning classic leadership responsibilities such as motivation, organizational strategy, and people development, to someone with more extensive general management experience and authentic interest in these areas. Avoid treating leadership like something that is superfluous based on having a self-managing staff. Consider designing a role under your direction that is solely accountable for these critical areas.

Process	• **Identify a sounding board/advisor:** Although you may prefer perfection and finding the "right" answer yourself, you should try to make decisions that take all factors and implications into consideration. It helps to employ the help of a counterpart from outside of your area as a sounding board to ensure that you are attuned to all possible dynamics and longer term implications of your decisions.
	• **Institute a recognition program:** Because you are not likely to naturally focus on ensuring that your staff feels valued, put a formalized recognition program in place that will force you to take time to determine specific people who deserve recognition. Delegate administration of the program to someone on your staff who will ensure it is implemented and fully utilized on a regular basis.
	• **Utilize ambassadors to broadcast your perspective:** Since you are potentially involved in complex and technical work that is unfamiliar to most of the organization at-large, it may help to identify communication experts and other leaders who can help ensure that others understand your views, conclusions, and recommendations. The challenge for Gurus is often being able to communicate a complex message in layman's terms, but doing so is critical for credibility and impact.

Process (cont'd)	• **Meeting management:** Consider incorporating the following prescriptions into how you plan and run your meetings:
	o Identify someone else to run the meeting—join only for the portion that is most critical for you to attend.
	o Schedule longer meetings that occur less frequently (e.g., monthly instead of weekly, with email communication as needed in between).
	o Utilize a trained meeting planner to help plan and orchestrate large and important meetings.
	o Institutionalize a norm at every meeting where participants need to do an informal "check in" to let everyone know how they are doing generally, before just moving immediately into the meeting agenda. Also, consider simple, lighthearted exercises such as a humorous or provocative question that everyone needs to respond to before officially starting the agenda.
People	• **Create role(s) to handle classic management areas:** Your staff should have consistent access to the full range of managerial support, with or without your direct involvement. Retain others to focus on leadership, talent development, motivation, and alignment with organizational goals. This could be in the form of assigning certain direct reports an additional role to handle certain issues such as training and development, motivational events for the team, and talent planning. You will still need to provide broad oversight, but more focused attention can be provided by others on a daily basis.

People (cont'd)	• **Appoint someone to take the temperature in your group:** Because you are not as likely to naturally take note of how people in your organization are feeling, identify a particular direct report or other leader who can essentially be your eyes and ears. This person is accountable to keep tabs on the motivational environment and regularly come up with ideas and recommendations for what might need to be done to keep the climate positive (e.g., teambuilding off-site events, departmental dinners, etc.).
Culture	In addition to the norms that are naturally aligned with the Guru's strengths, you should also consider emphasizing the following set of norms within your team: • **Teamwork and inclusivity:** Be sure that the staff feels like a team rather than a collection of individual contributors. Updates and information about key cross-functional initiatives should be shared as widely as possible, and not simply on a "need to know" basis. • **Celebrate success:** Individual and collective achievements should be recognized and celebrated. Accomplishments should not be taken for granted, and the team should be given opportunities to feel rewarded for their efforts, both big and small. • **Develop others:** Spend time helping less experienced staff members establish and pursue their career goals. Reward your staff for their efforts to teach and coach less experienced members. • **Respect for others:** Demonstrate an appreciation for the value that others provide to the organization beyond credentials or depth of subject matter expertise.

Jolie's Story Continued

Jolie, convinced that she should step up to help provide the leadership the organization needed, decided to have a teambuilding retreat with all eight of her direct reports. When they heard about the session, most of them were against it, fearing an awkward debacle. Because her leadership skills were not yet improved, she did not try to persuade them, but simply mandated that they attend. Despite the grumbling this produced within her department, Jolie proceeded with the teambuilding retreat.

At the beginning of the retreat, none of her employees spoke up. These highly paid and seasoned individuals were afraid to confront Jolie about the stressful work environment. Eventually, the facilitator managed to create a non-threatening climate that encouraged participation. Jolie's staff began to talk about their mixed experiences working in the department, and about how they suspected others within the organization felt about their group. Jolie was shocked by the emotions that her team was expressing, and felt guilty because she was completely unaware of the difficulties that her lack of leadership caused.

After the session, the first thing Jolie did was to institute regular staff meetings in which she rotated responsibilities for the agenda and facilitation amongst her direct reports. These staff meetings helped to break down silos and provided an opportunity for her employees to get to know each other better. In addition, because she knew about her own leadership deficiencies and tendencies, she decided to give one of her direct reports the role of leading a departmental effort to more rigorously evaluate and assess talent for future leadership opportunities. Over time, Jolie began to completely reformulate what success meant in the department, both for herself and others. Technical capabilities would always be important; however, she now required her employees to add complementary skill sets to encourage more well-rounded development. Jolie and the designated direct report worked with Human Resources to outline a competency model that reflected the full complement of what would be required for advancement within the group, and Jolie used the model religiously to help keep her honest and on track in terms of identifying future talent. With these efforts in place, Jolie began to feel a different mood emerge in her group over time. She was hopeful that her concerted efforts to better leverage people and processes would help to minimize and perhaps even disguise her own natural tendencies.

Wisdom for Gurus

Most organizations will seek out and covet Gurus because they provide the intellectual power and depth of understanding that separate the best from the rest. In many organizations, the Guru is considered a thought leader who is not expected to demonstrate traditional leadership capabilities. Gurus must often recognize for themselves the importance of providing leadership, even among other smart people. Everyone wants to feel like they matter. Employees, no matter how capable they are, typically want access to their boss, feedback on how they are doing, and some semblance of guidance and direction toward collective goals.

As a leader, you are likely to be faced with unique challenges and dynamics in navigating your way through fundamental leadership responsibilities and classic leadership events. Like many things in life, if you are insightful about how you respond to certain situations, you are in a much better position to self-manage in a way that will allow you to be most effective. What follows is specific advice for Gurus in the following situations:

1. *Making an Impact as a Leader*
2. *Managing and Developing Others*
3. *Relationship Building*
4. *Getting Promoted*
5. *Moving On from the Organization*

Making an Impact as a Guru

Making an impact is about getting yourself and your work noticed in the organization. It is about developing a positive reputation in the minds of others as someone who has the wherewithal to make things happen and improve the organization and its people in some way. Gurus are often challenged in particular ways in this area.

As a Guru, you are likely to assume that your excellent work will have the impact you desire and should stand on its own merit. Gurus have a tendency to present information to the organization without running it through the filter of the organization's goals, politics, or values. If you want to be impactful as a Guru, you must consider your audience and determine the most effective way to get your message across. It might not be a bad idea to ask for assistance from other leaders in the organization as to how best to present your ideas. They might suggest that you try to find common ground by using analogies, or recommend that you use language that is more appropriate for non-experts.

To make the greatest impact, you should present yourself as a member of the team as opposed to being an objective observer. Many

Gurus fall into the habit of criticizing the work of others. In your pursuit of the absolute truth or best answer, you may inadvertently alienate your colleagues who may be less accustomed to the rigor of your critical thinking process. By way of example, James, a VP in a large retail organization, was hired because of his extensive knowledge of global markets. But whenever others in the company tried to come to him with new concepts he would systematically dismantle their ideas. James hoped that if his colleagues' ideas had merit, they would defend their rationale and persuade him. In reality, James' colleagues felt that he was condescending and arrogant, which led them to stop bringing him new ideas. For Gurus, making an impact means being able to demonstrate your value by sharing your expertise (which is what you were hired to do, after all) in a way that empowers those around you, and does not stand in judgment of others.

Managing Others as a Guru

A key element of any leadership role is that of managing and developing talent, and each style is challenged by different aspects of this area of responsibility.

As a Guru, you naturally believe that your direct reports should be self-managing. Therefore, you tend to select and work most easily with people who do not need close oversight. Additionally, you are more likely to focus your efforts to develop others strictly on technical expertise—without sufficient attention to the full range of competencies that may in fact be important long term. James, for instance, was eager to teach his people about global markets, but neglected all other areas of development that might actually turn them into future leaders. To grow leadership talent effectively, you need to develop the *whole* person—even if that means trying to develop others in areas you are not particularly good at yourself.

As a Guru, you are likely to want to see only the finished product from your people, and consequences follow when they don't achieve good results. Unfortunately though, this hands-off approach is not an effective way to help others develop professionally. You should actively engage yourself as the leader and see developing others as a core part of your responsibility, not something that will just happen magically. You need to regularly assess others' skills and development needs, and empower them to take advantage of development opportunities both inside and outside of the organization. Let them know that you are a key resource in helping to guide and support their development, clarifying available resources and taking time to point them in the right direction. At the same time, it is important that you make them understand that they are also accountable to be an active partner in the development process.

Building Relationships as a Guru

Building and maintaining productive working relationships is a key ingredient for the success of every leader and manager. Here is some perspective about the typical dynamics Gurus face in developing effective relationships, and some practical advice and guidance to help things along.

Based on the focused and intense nature of your role, you may prefer to work independently. However, it's unproductive and self-destructive to become a loner within an organization. You will need to invite others into your world, because your natural style, despite what may actually be true about you, may be signaling "Do Not Disturb" to those around you. You can minimize this perception by having internal conferences, meetings, or workshops to talk about your work projects and your goals.

Your preference for solitude can appear insensitive and uncaring to others. In reality, it's merely a matter of concentration and deep thought. Gurus are so focused on their goals and areas of interest, they often lose sight of the world around them—which is not always a bad thing. A scientist pursuing a cure for a rare disease may think "I don't care if you like me, I don't care how you treat me, and I don't care how I treat you. The work I'm doing is more important." And to a certain extent, they're right. We want that scientist to find a cure. But in the atmosphere of a more typical work setting, isolation is not always practical, especially if you're responsible for leading a team.

Relationship building is never going to be your strong point. And it doesn't have to be. In fact, many organizations give their gurus a "pass" in this area—they don't expect them to show up at the company's social functions, for example. No one expects you to take your staff to a baseball game or to hang out for drinks after work. But it is possible for you to take smaller steps by building relationships based on shared interests and shared results.

Getting Promoted as a Guru

Each style has a unique set of dynamics when it comes to trying to get promoted and dealing with the realities of not having received the promotion they thought they were deserving of. Here are a few pointers for Gurus.

If you are a Guru, you're probably not as enamored with promotions as most leadership types. You are likely to believe that people should be organized based on their depth of expertise rather than their leadership capabilities. You want most to have the control and freedom to work the way you want. However, promotions are one of the few ways to get that power and control. Ultimately, becoming a leader will be essential to getting your work done. You will be in a position to develop other leaders who can support your agenda and to encourage organizational values that will keep your work relevant. As a Guru, you may be thinking too narrowly about positions from which you can impact the organization. You may only envision yourself within your domain of expertise. However, a broader position can get you more influence to drive what is most important to you. Consider other places or roles from which you could make a difference with your expertise. Suggest to your organization the possibility of creating a thought leadership role where you would be responsible for persuading and influencing others regarding the ideas and results that come from your work, rather than focusing on more traditional leadership functions like motivation and direction setting.

Take some time to imagine the possibilities—being a leader and an expert are not mutually exclusive. Don't avoid promotions just because they take you out of your domain. You might find a leadership role exciting, and an opportunity to enrich your expertise in other areas. You may have to take a leap of faith, leaving behind the idea that you need empirical evidence that you can be competent in different type of job. Don't define yourself so narrowly. Keep in mind that even Gurus can evolve.

Moving on as a Guru

At some point or another in your leadership career, you may find yourself having to move on from an organization. If so, you might find the following insights and advice meaningful to ensure that you are able to keep things in a healthy perspective.

Gurus tend to have minimum difficulty moving on because they can take their most important characteristic, their expertise, with them. However, because organizations allow Gurus to segregate themselves, you may become complacent and miss opportunities to advance your expertise inside or outside of the organization. In fact, you might not even know that your area of expertise is being devalued by the organization unless someone tells you. Keep an eye on changes in the amount of interest superiors show in your work, the availability of resources (including staff), and any changes that make your work life more difficult. These are typically signs that what you have to offer may no longer be of value and it is time to move on.

Jolie's Story Continued

A year later, Jolie brought her team together for another off-site to get the group out of the weeds and focused on the kinds of things that were important to the group's overall health. While it was the external consultant who pushed her to commit to this kind of meeting, Jolie realized afterwards how needed it in fact was. The first part of the meeting focused on developing future bench strength, given that a few key senior level people in the group had decided to take early retirement packages based on a company restructuring, and key roles needed to be filled right away. Given the experiences her direct reports had had with one another throughout the year with the new meeting format that was introduced by Jolie, the conversations flowed freely and the group spoke about the talent in the organization in a lively and thoughtful manner. Jolie participated in the discussions as was needed given her role, but mostly sat back and admired what was happening in front of her—a group of individuals who had in fact evolved during the past year into a cohesive, high performing team helping shape important decisions regarding the future of the department. Jolie (with a helpful nudge from the external facilitator) had arranged for the group to do a surprise off-site dinner experience that involved small teams working together to prepare and eat a meal. The group had a blast and everyone talked about their time together in a way that made Jolie come across like the energizing, motivational leader that she usually just admired from afar.

A few days later when Jolie found herself at her desk well into the evening, an email popped up from her manager, with a cc: to his boss. While only a few lines long, the email applauded Jolie's recent efforts and ability to develop a strong team that appeared well positioned to take on future challenges ahead. He commented that he had run into a few members of the team who raved about the meeting and spoke about how excited they were to be a part of Jolie's team. The email was a perfect ending to a long day.

Chapter 7

The Stabilizer
Making Sure the Trains Are on Time

A re you a Stabilizer? Start by taking a few minutes to complete the following brief symptom questionnaire.

Please read each of the following statements. Using the scale provided, rate the extent to which each symptom applies to you. Total your score by adding up your ratings on individual items. Determine the extent to which this leadership style is reflective of your tendencies based on the final scoring provided.

Rating Scale

1 = This statement hardly describe me
2 = This statement somewhat describes me
3 = This statement definitely describes me

	Please indicate the extent to which each statement describes you.	Little Extent	Some Extent	Great Extent
1.	I believe everyone should be held to the same standards with no exceptions	1	2	3
2.	I believe that people should accept their assignments, without much questioning	1	2	3
3.	I regularly follow up with others to ensure accountability and follow-through	1	2	3

4.	I always try to deliver precisely what was asked of me even when it doesn't make perfect sense	1	2	3
5.	I create rules and processes for myself and others to follow in order to ensure consistency	1	2	3
6.	I prefer predictability and dislike surprises	1	2	3
	Total Score			

Total Score	Description
16–18	This is very likely your leadership type
12–15	This may be your leadership type, but you likely demonstrate other types as well
6–11	This is not likely your leadership type

Carl's Story

Carl is a well-regarded manager of the logistics department of a company that distributes books to major bookstores throughout the country and internationally. He is best known in the organization for his reliability, dependability, and focus on managing the performance of others. He is a tidy man in both his dress and the way he manages his environment. Carl's office is immaculate. His desk is always clean, with pictures of his family placed appropriately to the right hand side. He answers all of his emails promptly and cleans out his email box daily. When Carl meets with his boss, he arrives with pen and paper in hand, poised to write down directions and instructions. He does not want to disappoint his boss Gary, so he tries to do everything exactly as Gary instructs him to do. By most measures of success regarding logistics, Carl is considered successful. Recently, the company acquired another book distributor and doubled its capacity. However, Carl was not promoted to the senior job that emerged as a result of the acquisition. He was shocked, hurt, and confused as to why he was found to be an unsuitable candidate for the bigger, more challenging job. Carl felt betrayed by his boss, but was too scared to consider any alternatives. When he asked for feedback, he was told that he was a good administrator but not the type of leader the company needs given the changes in the world of books, particularly given the dominance of on-line book sellers. Carl remained in his current role, reporting to a new boss, in a newly created position responsible for company-wide logistics.

Carl felt he needed to do something and remembered that several of the other executives used executive coaches to help them get ahead. He decided to give it a try because he wanted to know how he'd missed the cues, and what he could do to change that perception and be considered for broader responsibilities in the future. His coach suggested that he take a look at the environment he'd created to determine a prescription that would help him to outsmart his leadership deficiencies.

Understanding the Style

If you are a Stabilizer, you are someone who is interested in keeping the organization in tip-top shape as defined by your superiors. You are smart and efficient and strive for flawless execution. You want everything in order and usually tend to play it safe. You are not likely to focus much on the future or nuances of life in the organization, in large part because it is difficult to get your arms around them—and you are a person who gravitates toward clarity and certainty. It's not likely that you will risk expected results by developing creative ideas that might get you more than expected. You usually feel it's better to stick with the tried and true ways of doing things.

You are most comfortable when you know what is expected, and you will work tirelessly with a positive attitude to achieve results. Uncomfortable with ambiguity, you will tend to avoid setting risky goals and objectives. Carl's response to work difficulties, for example, was to determine and implement processes and procedures to make things clearer and more efficient. He looked to his boss to provide the direction and insight that was required, wanting the certainty of avoiding the downside of another mistake.

As a Stabilizer, you are pleasant and can develop friendly relationships with others. However, you put clear boundaries around your relationships at work, and actually prefer to have friendships outside of the organization so that you do not have to feel conflicted when managing and monitoring the performance of others. While this makes things easier in many ways, this tendency can also make it difficult for others to connect with you in a meaningful way. Ultimately, the lack of connection results in the loss of many opportunities to become more aware of what is really going on in the department and how others are feeling.

You're comfortable being in charge, especially because it gives you the control you need to achieve and maintain consistent results. You demonstrate the authority described in your position. If you feel like you do not have the authority to make a decision, then you won't. You seek advice and guidance from others, since being cautious has paid off in the past. You expect the people you manage to come to you if they need assistance, otherwise you assume that all is well. However, if staff members need assistance, you will make it a priority to provide the necessary training, development, experiences etc. to help ensure their success. While you are not known to be particularly motivational, you feel responsible for the development and career plans of others.

You like to focus on developing and maintaining proper systems and protocols to focus your staff's behavior. You are available and accessible, and make sure that you provide communication processes and opportunities to keep everyone informed. While you can participate in conversations regarding the future, you are not likely to act until you are given permission to do so. As a Stabilizer, you are recognized and rewarded for being predictable and consistent, and you are the smart choice for a mature and well developed business and/or staff. To become a complete leader, however, you need to put more emphases on pushing the limits, becoming more inspiring and motivational, and engaging in more forward thinking activities.

Summary of the Style
Strengths

- Demonstrates a strong and disciplined approach to planning and organizing
- Monitors and controls the performance of others, and holds them accountable
- Typically has reputation as being very reliable and dependable
- Builds and maintains positive work relationships

Challenges

- Low risk orientation—seeks predictability
- Often uncomfortable with ambiguity and changing priorities
- Avoids questioning assignments and authority
- More focused on today rather than the future
- Does not take active role in truly developing others' long term careers

Prescriptions for This Style

If the story and/or the descriptors of the Stabilizer resonate with you, consider the following prescriptions as practical tactics and approaches for outsmarting your leadership genes. Review the list in its entirety first, then go back and consider the relevance and appropriateness of each particular item. Make notes in the margins to indicate which of the prescriptions might be worthwhile to incorporate into your plan.

LEADERSHIP PRESCRIPTIONS FOR THE STABILIZER

Environmental Element	Prescriptions To Consider
Structure	• **Select a seasoned team:** Regardless of the size of your staff, you will be most successful managing a group of experienced professionals who do not require substantial development effort on your part. If you do have junior staffers, assign more seasoned team members who are comfortable with coaching to help them along. • **Seek access to the informal organizational structure:** To balance your preference for formal work and reporting relationships, it is important to stay connected to what is happening outside of your direct area of responsibility. Form relationships with your boss, cross-functional peers, and possibly external consultants to ensure that you are truly "in the know" about informal organizational happenings. While it may not be your nature to focus on the political dynamics, you need to know about them because you may very well be impacted by them at some point in the future.
Process	• **Determine when decisions can be made independently:** You may feel most comfortable making policy-driven determinations, and yet seek input from others when dealing with new and/or future-oriented decisions that are ambiguous or uncertain. However, making collaborative decisions is not always appropriate or efficient. Therefore, you should first identify decisions that can be made unilaterally, and then begin making small decisions independently to build your tolerance for risk over time. Every time a decision needs to be made, make it a point to critically analyze whether an independent or collaborative approach is optimal.

Process
(cont'd)
	• **Develop opportunities for cross-functional communication:** Your preference for clarity and well-defined roles may inhibit your communication across boundaries - simply because the more people that are involved in something the murkier goals and roles can get. To prevent work silos from emerging, create processes and norms to enable your team to interact with other business areas on a regular basis—even in the absence of a particular goal or project that requires interaction. Initiate round table discussions, for example, to encourage sharing across groups, so that best practices can be determined and resources leveraged. Doing so in the absence of a particular goal or project will help solidify a foundation of relationships—making it easier when something tangible does need to be accomplished.
	
	• **Allow for spontaneous and informal communication:** It is important to allow ideas to take shape outside of formal gatherings, even though this may not be your own personal preference. This includes encouraging direct reports to meet in your absence, or through virtual media such as a corporate intranet.
	
	• **Meeting management:** Consider incorporating the following prescriptions into how you plan and run your meetings:
	
	  o Bookend the formal agenda with unstructured social time for the group.
	
	  o Build in time for icebreaker type exercises to warm the group up before getting down to business.
	
	  o Invite guests in to shake things up and change up what is probably a predictable event.

Process (cont'd)	o Spend time talking about what is on people's minds before starting your formal agenda. (e.g., "What I am thinking about coming into today's meeting is . . .")
	o Make sure meeting time is focused on substantive and challenging issues that truly require discussion and debate—do not limit your meetings to discussion of administrative issues and project updates (these can be handled off line in many cases).
People	• **Develop recognition programs for creative, innovative, and future-oriented ideas:** It is important to publicly reward sought-after behaviors, even though they may not be consistent with your personal strengths as a leader. Your staff should feel encouraged to make such contributions in a variety of settings, including one-on-one, group conversations, team meetings, and informal discussions.
	• **Maintain an active succession plan for your staff:** Because leaders with the Stabilizer style tend to focus on maintaining consistency and order, they can often be caught off guard by unpredictable events, such as the sudden departure of a key team member. It is important to proactively identify who is going to replace whom, and to have an ongoing network to supply new talent if and when the situation occurs.
	• **Focus on creating a motivational climate:** Consider forming an ad hoc committee tasked with motivating the staff. Give them free reign and responsibility (within appropriate limits) to design and implement initiatives that they believe will appeal to a majority of the staff, and make a personal commitment to support their ideas if they are within reason (even if you don't personally think they are necessary).

Culture	In addition to the norms that are naturally aligned with the Stabilizer's strengths, you should also consider emphasizing the following set of norms within your team:
	• **Tolerance:** Use mistakes as learning opportunities. Allow differences of opinion to emerge and play out before seeking conformity.
	• **Flexibility:** Demonstrate openness to new ideas and ways of doing things.
	• **Collaboration:** Encourage teamwork and cross-functional communication. Avoid seeing people and functions as self-contained entities.
	• **Team Identity:** Create a unique team identity that will set the group apart from others in the organization.

Carl's Story Continued

With the help of guidance from his executive coach, Carl created a two-year plan regarding how he would use his environment to outsmart his leadership deficiencies. Mostly, Carl wanted to prove to Gary that he was capable of handling a larger, more complex organization. He decided to change his approach to status update meetings he had with his boss. In the past, he would take lots of data and a few of his direct reports with him to the meeting. Now, prior to meetings with Gary, Carl sends him a summary of all of his projects so that if questions do arise, they can be discussed during the first part of meeting. The remainder of the meeting is now used to discuss how his department can support broader efforts of the organization. For example, since the company is going more global, what can his department do to support this initiative longer-term? Also, Carl no longer hesitates to talk openly with his boss about things that concern him.

By taking the risk and becoming more vulnerable, Carl was able to become a better leader. Meetings with his boss are now more future-oriented. They are also more of a dialogue and exchange of perspectives, rather than simply a time for Carl to receive directives and provide project updates. Slowly but surely, Carl began to feel a more positive vibe with Gary, and Gary began to incrementally give Carl some opportunities to be more visible in the organization. Carl was hopeful and optimistic about where this might lead.

Wisdom for Stabilizers

In order for you to advance, you will need to be able to keep up with the changes in the business environment and demonstrate the initiative required to maintain a competitive advantage. You will also need to nurture and develop talent in your organization in order to bring energy and new ideas to the work culture. The best way for you to do this is to create an environment where you maintain results, keep an eye on the future, and develop rather than monitor performance of others. You should become more thoughtful about challenges in the business and be proactive about offering solutions. In addition, you should provide your subordinates with more leeway to do things their way and accept the fact that mistakes can happen. Odd as it may seem to you, these actions will likely lead to not only individual growth and development, but also improvement in results.

As a leader, you are likely to be faced with unique challenges and dynamics in navigating your way through classic leadership responsibilities and particular leadership events. Like many things in life, if you are insightful about how you typically respond to certain situations, you are in a much better position to self-manage in a way that will allow you to be most effective. What follows is specific advice for Stabilizers for the following situations:

1. *Making an Impact as a Leader*
2. *Managing and Developing Others*
3. *Relationship Building*
4. *Getting Promoted*
5. *Moving On from the Organization*

Making an Impact as a Stabilizer

Making an impact is about getting yourself and your work noticed in the organization. It is about developing a positive reputation in the minds of others as someone who has the wherewithal to make things happen and improve the organization and its people in some way. Stabilizers are often challenged in particular ways in this area.

You feel successful and impactful when everything on your to-do list has been accomplished. You likely have no need to tell anyone else about it, as completing your list is a reward unto itself. However, others will not necessarily experience your impact in the same way. For the sake of your career, someone needs to know about your accomplishments. For example, you may have implemented a program that has reduced the number of workplace accidents by 60%—but you never got credit for it. You can get the support you need to do more beneficial work for the organization if others clearly see your contributions. The more they know about who you are and what you do, the more impactful you will become. So, get out of your office and meet your peers in other parts of the organization. When your peers find out what you've done and how it has impacted the organization, they will become your personal ambassadors and advocates. There is no need to brag. Modesty may be a virtue, however, being modest is very different than being invisible.

Managing Others as a Stabilizer

A key element of any leadership role is that of managing and developing talent, and each style is challenged by different aspects of this area of responsibility.

People bring a variety of assets to every organization. Some assets have to do with the tasks individuals perform, some of it has to do with relationship building, some of it has to do with understanding organizational dynamics. Stabilizers tend to supervise the tasks or activities of their staff rather than to manage the people themselves. As a Stabilizer, you may think you're being a good manager when you encourage your people to fulfill their tasks. For instance, Dave, a Stabilizer we know, is more likely to look at his employee Andrew and say, "Did Andrew accomplish everything on his list of things to do?" rather than managing Andrew's full work experience, including his relationship-building skills and overall career development. Dave is simply managing Andrew's day-to-day activities as needs arise in the organization. At the beginning of each year, Dave is likely to set activity objectives for each of his staff and then "manage" them throughout the year to help them meet these objectives. He's not taking into account the value each person brings to the organization.

Management requires that you think more about the future and how it will impact you and your employees. If you stay focused solely on the present projects, you will miss opportunities to prepare and deploy your direct reports to meet the needs of the future. Ultimately, that will undermine their ability to compete and advance in the organization. Directing and supervising employees' activities in the present is very important. However, this will not ultimately be sufficient to have others view you as a leader who can truly take on a broader level of responsibility for others.

Building Relationships as a Stabilizer

Building and maintaining productive working relationships is a key ingredient for the success of every leader and manager. Technical expertise and smarts are in many ways a foregone conclusion. Here is some perspective about the typical dynamics Stabilizers face in developing effective relationships, and practical advice and guidance to help things along where needed.

You tend to build and maintain positive relationships with other people because you adhere to appropriate relationship boundaries. You don't ask questions that are too personal or invite others to ask the same of you. You make it clear that relationships should be built to help ensure that organizational goals can be achieved. This can make you appear aloof and some personality types may have trouble connecting to you. Keep in mind that it is good to have a variety of types of relationships in the work environment, and in fact it might benefit you to do so. There may be some people with whom you share interests and hobbies outside the scope of work. It is often beneficial to talk about those things as a foundation for building familiarity and trust - especially when you are working on a high profile project or having to work through a difficult and challenging set of circumstances.

Getting Promoted as a Stabilizer

Each style has a unique set of dynamics when it comes to trying to get promoted and dealing with the realities of not having received the promotion they thought they were deserving of. Here are a few pointers for Stabilizers.

As a Stabilizer, you are likely to ask "How *do* you get promoted in this organization?" Once you get a clear understanding of the process and criteria, you set out to follow the prescribed steps. But, as you look around, you may find that others are getting promoted outside of the process. Your initial response will typically be "But that's not fair!" When it comes to getting promoted, your primary challenge will be to recognize that there are informal realities such as "who you know" and "who knows you." You will need to spend as much time focusing on getting to know and understand these informal processes and norms as you do the formal processes in order to determine your real chances of getting promoted. This may mean spending more time networking with key influencers in your organization—perhaps more than you may be personally comfortable doing. But if you don't step out of your comfort zone, you may never get the chance to step out of your current position.

Moving on as a Stabilizer

At some point or another in your leadership career, you may find yourself having to move on from an organization. If so, you might find the following insights and advice meaningful to ensure that you are able to keep things in a healthy perspective.

Since there are typically no organization policies and procedures to tell anyone when it's time to move on, Stabilizers run the risk of being surprised when they are ultimately asked to do so. It is important for you to read the organizational cues, such as not being invited to key meetings, having seemingly good ideas dismissed out of hand, not getting selected for unique and forward-thinking projects, etc. While occasional events such as these may simply be isolated incidents with no underlying implications, multiple events like these may be indicators that you are no longer in favor within the organization. The challenge for you as a Stabilizer is to pay closer attention to these kinds of events and to talk to trusted advisors if you are concerned that your job may be in jeopardy. Stay on top of the "soft" skills like relationship building and office politics. You may believe that if you do your job well, you will be treated fairly. But organizations do not always live by the rules; surprising things happen all the time. Do not let yourself be blindsided by suddenly being let go without having had any idea you were at risk in the first place.

And remember that as a Stabilizer, you have the built-in skill set to get back on your feet. You have a natural ability to plan and get yourself organized, which is exactly what you need when looking for a new position.

Carl's Story Continued

A year later, when the organization acquired a new company, Carl was invited to present recommendations from a global taskforce that was formed to plan for effective ways to manage the merger. While Carl was a bit nervous, he was well prepared for his presentation and was excited about the chance to interact at this more senior level. With advice from his coach, he also realized that part of his effectiveness and impact would depend on his ability to engage the group in meaningful conversation about their perspectives on the recommendations, rather than to feel like everything had to be fully vetted. Carl also realized that his nervous energy was actually healthy. For the first time in as long as he could remember, he felt authentically passionate about some of the ideas and strategies proposed—even if they did not all make it to the final round.

After the presentation, Carl and Gary agreed to meet for a drink to debrief. Carl was confident and excited about how things had gone and was hopeful that Gary would feel the same. He was relieved to get very positive feedback. The audience approved of many of the taskforce's ideas, and they particularly appreciated Carl's energy and enthusiasm.

The conversation transitioned to a more general one about how things had been going at work, and Gary offered unsolicited feedback about the fact that he had thoroughly enjoyed working with Carl over the last several months—that he appreciated Carl's broader level of thinking because it challenged him to do the same. Gary introduced the idea of Carl delegating some of his day-to-day duties to his staff so that he could free up time to head another project of strategic importance. While he had to contain his excitement in the moment so he did not come off as too junior, Carl was thrilled at the opportunity. He could hardly wait to call his coach to thank him for his help and talk about how to take things even further. Most of all, he began to feel more confident that he did not have to change the core of his being in order to grow in his career.

Chapter 8

Implementing Prescriptions

There comes a point in every leader's life when you know that changes must be made. Maybe a business crisis has pushed you to the point where the survival of the organization is at stake. Perhaps the crisis is more of a personal nature and it's your own survival within the organization that's in jeopardy. Or maybe it's your own insight that tells you you're in a rut and that it is time to find your way to a new opportunity. It doesn't really matter how you got to this point. What's important is that you listen to the signs and signals around you and get moving.

That's what this book has been about. No matter what style of leader you are, the message is the same. Understanding who you are, understanding your environment, and maximizing both is critical. If you want something different to happen, look in different places for the answers. As is the case with medical prescriptions, if you go off your hypertension diet and eat lots of salt the result will be higher blood pressure readings. Consequently, you need to make sure that you either stick to your doctor's orders or make a concerted effort to try something else in order to yield a different result.

However, there are certain things that need to be taken into consideration when you make the decision to follow any particular prescription. If the doctor tells you to start exercising, you can't just go home, jump on a treadmill, and jog for an hour on the first day. If you do so, you will surely come away exhausted and full of aches and pains, and likely decide in that moment that it wasn't worth the effort after all. So it is with implementing any of the prescriptions we have suggested in this book. There are real-world issues to consider before taking any action, and the more preparation and planning you do before you get started, the fewer issues you will encounter.

The Implementation Process

In order to maximize effectiveness and impact, there are five steps to take in the process of implementing any of the leadership prescriptions you find in this book.

1. *Be Aware of Your Surroundings*
2. *Make a Plan*
3. *Communicate the Plan*
4. *Implement the Plan*
5. *Collect Feedback*

1. Be Aware of Your Surroundings

After you have chosen a prescription that fits your style, your next step is to ensure that what you have chosen is realistic, practical, and appropriate under your particular set of circumstances. Here are some important questions to ask yourself:

Category	Questions To Ask Yourself
Support and Resources Required	• Whose help will I need to make this work? • Can I get support for this prescription from my boss if his or her approval is necessary? • What are the resources required to follow this prescription in terms of time and money? • How much of my own time and commitment is it going to take to get this implemented? • Is this a quick hit or is it something that will take concerted effort over a period of time? • Is this prescription realistic based on my current set of circumstances?
How Well My Changes Fit Culturally	• Can I get support for this prescription from my boss if his or her approval is necessary? • Will the resistance from senior management or my employees be too severe? Is there another way to do this that will land more softly? • Is this going to be a challenge to implement, given the culture of my organization? • How can I prepare the organization to avoid culture shock related to my new ways?
How My Change Will Impact Others	• Who is this going to impact most and what can I do to get them ready for the change? • Have I thought through the possible consequences so my intent does not backfire? • Will my plans affect other departments, and if so how?

Communication Issues That Need to Be Considered	• What's the best way to communicate this to others, if at all? • Do I know exactly who needs to be told about the plans? • When do I need to communicate my plans?
Summary Question	• How do I feel about the answers to these questions?

The last summary question, while answered partially through your gut feeling, is extremely important. If, after you have answered all of the prior questions, you feel positive and confident about your answers, then you should move forward with your selected prescription. If you are only moderately comfortable and confident in your responses, then move ahead in small steps. If you are uncomfortable or unsure about more than a few of your prior answers, then perhaps this is not the right prescription for you at this time. Move on to the next one on your list, and conduct a similar litmus test until you feel comfortable enough to move ahead.

The Realities of Side Effects

We all know that the side effects of certain medications, while not typical, can be worse than the actual ailment you took the medication for in the first place. The same is true with our leadership prescriptions, because your actions are often interconnected to other people and processes in the organization. For example, if you decide to promote a direct report to be your formal Chief of Staff, other people might say, "Why not me?" A neighboring department might say, "Why do you get a Chief of Staff and we don't?" Human

Resources may complain that you didn't work through them to add the new role to the current job accountabilities.

It is always important to keep the organizational culture, policies, conventions and protocol in mind. Just because a change makes sense to you and may have worked in a former work environment, don't assume a similar change can be implemented in your current environment without consequences. For example, Annette, a senior level leader in a medium-sized non-profit organization, became enthralled with the idea of having only a few direct reports, because she knew she was introverted by nature and would be overwhelmed by many direct reports. It worked out amazingly well in this organization, where the Human Resources department was fairly unsophisticated and hands-off in matters at the individual department level. She made the desired changes and went from seven to three direct reports without considerable disruption. A few years later she found herself in a much larger, more complex corporation. When she proposed the same reorganization, she received a great deal of push-back from her new boss who questioned how it would impact those tenured staff who would no longer have direct access to her as the senior leader. Ultimately, she needed to give up on that idea and try other prescriptions that would achieve the same goal, since it was certainly not worth risking her reputation as a new leader. Annette really hadn't considered the possible consequences of this prescription in her new situation. The simple truth is that careful planning and consideration of the specific context will go a long way to ensuring success (see Figure 4).

Figure 4

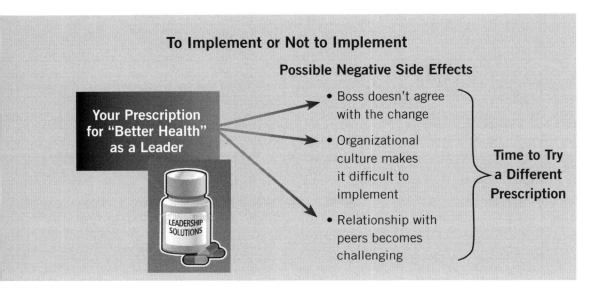

Positive Side Effects

As many people have discovered when taking a new medication, not all side effects are negative. Maybe you are taking medication to treat a pre-diabetic condition and you are lucky enough to lose a few pounds in the process. Perhaps your doctor has prescribed blood pressure medication and you have noticed that you feel an increase in your energy level. The same is true for prescriptions you might put in place to address your leadership tendencies, which is what happened to Mike, a Vice President of a small insurance company a few years back. Mike was highly regarded as someone who delivered exceptional results at every turn, but was often frustrated by the fact that he was unable to keep up with the rapidly changing insurance market. He used to attend conferences and external events regularly, but was finding it more and more difficult to find the time. He considered delegating more to his new staff, but did not feel comfortable that they would be able to perform the work to his high standards. However, Mike finally realized that, given his Guru leadership style, delegating to appropriate staff members was probably the best option. He handed over leadership of a large, time-sensitive client project to a young woman named Karen, who had recently joined his team. While it was slow going at first, over time he gave Karen more aspects of the project, and eventually added others to the effort. Doing so allowed Mike to focus on other external issues once again. Mike's boss was supportive of the idea, because he knew how critical it was for Mike to remain current in the field.

A few months later, Mike was excited about how "free" he was feeling—and how energizing it was to be out and about again. He admitted that while his original intent was simply to delegate this project so that his time was freed up to do other things, the result was a huge positive benefit for Karen. Mike's boss was not only singing Karen's praises, he commended Mike for fostering her growth both professionally and personally! While it had only been six months since she joined the organization, Mike was contemplating promoting Karen at the end of the year if she continued to show similar development progress.

This is just one example of many situations where leaders put new practices and processes in place in an attempt to enhance their own effectiveness, and end up positively impacting something else as a by-product. You might change the way you run your staff meetings by having members of your team present various hot topics of interest, and in the process you may develop someone's presentation skills and impact the overall motivational climate of the team. You might restructure the department so that you have fewer direct reports and can more easily focus externally. In the process you force the smaller number of direct reports to stretch themselves and their capabilities—which can in turn lead to them being better prepared for larger roles more quickly than might otherwise have been the case. And, you might just find that when one prescription is implemented well and applied with consistency, it eliminates the need for other prescriptions that you may have mapped out as a part of your overall plan (see Figure 5).

Figure 5

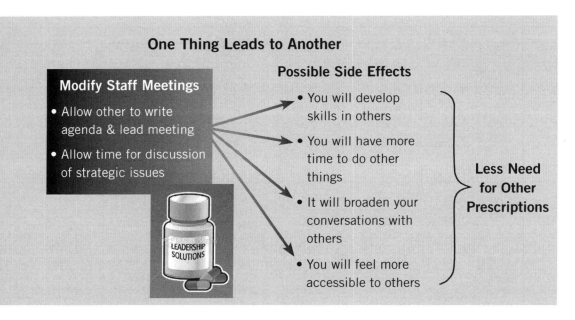

Possible side effects related to leadership prescriptions, both positive and negative, are important to consider as you think through what makes most sense for you. Just as you work with your doctor to find the best ways to manage your physical health and genetic predispositions, it's important that you think through the implications of choices you might make for your leadership prescription plan, so that you are as well informed as possible.

2. Make a Plan

Figure out your priorities. If you have answered all the questions on page 147, you should have the information you need to put your prescription(s) into action. Don't feel that you have to follow a prescription exactly the way we have written it. The prescriptions are intended to be used as a template which you may want to revise in order to fit your particular needs, including your organization's standards and culture. The prescription you choose should be one that is associated with your style, one for which you can receive needed support, and one that makes sense given the time restrictions and people with whom you work. Like any other medication, your leadership prescription may not sit well at first and may take some adjustments and tweaks before it begins to take effect and create the desired outcome.

Write out your plan so that you can be sure you have covered all bases and that it is clear and logical, especially if you're going to have to present it to your boss or other key colleagues. Make a list of the possible obstacles you might face in trying to implement your plan. Such obstacles might include:

- Other people in your department
- The organization's culture
- The current business climate
- People's resistance to change
- Lack of resources

This list is not an excuse to say that the plan cannot be done; rather, it's an acknowledgement of some realities you may encounter. Acknowledging them enables you to plan for them and proceed accordingly. Even if you can't do everything on your wish list right now, there is always something that can be done. You may have to proceed on a smaller scale than you originally intended, but if you persevere, you will eventually reach your goal. You have to do *something* to see different results.

3. Communicate the Plan

Make a list of all the parties that will be affected by putting your prescription into place. If you're going to change the way you run your weekly meetings, for example, you may only need to relay this change to the people who attend these meetings. If you want to change the organization chart, it is more likely to require more clear and careful messaging to key stakeholders (e.g., your boss, your boss's boss, Human Resources, etc.) before you can proceed. There may be employee policy implications to your plan, including job design, salary implications, and job leveling. As with any organizational change, the more significant the change and the more people impacted, the greater will be the need for thoughtful and deliberate communication. Be prepared to explain why you are making changes— what prompted the changes, how you are planning to make these changes, and what you expect to achieve as a result of making these changes. Compose a list of people with whom you think you should be communicating. Use your best judgment. Go over your list and ask yourself if there are any not-so-obvious staff members or colleagues who should be included. Then, for each person listed, ask yourself, "What is the risk of *not* telling this person?" As a general rule, it's typically better to over-communicate than to under-communicate.

4. Implement the Plan

Start small. Many times prescriptions fail because people try to implement large changes all at once. Most of the time, people really do want to change, but are afraid or resistant, especially if the change takes them out of their comfort zone or simply seems overwhelming. Like beginning an exercise regimen, you just need to get started by taking baby steps like walking the stairs instead of taking the elevator—or doing just 10 minutes on the treadmill 3 days a week for the first week and then building up gradually over time. If you're going to change the way you run your staff meetings, for example, you might want to begin by saying, "We're going to try it this way for a while and see what happens." Take one small step at a time. Start with something simple. Commit to your changes for a specific period of time—perhaps six months, or a year. Your goal should be to institutionalize the change in your work environment over time so that it becomes a natural way in which you work, but starting small and building can be the key to long term success.

5. Collect Feedback

Whatever change you are trying to implement will be a work in progress. You've got to keep revisiting your prescription the same way you would revisit your doctor for your yearly checkup. Things may have changed since you started the process. You may need to modify the prescription, or discard it altogether. You may need to add another "medication" to enhance the first one's effectiveness. Go back to the people you communicated with when you initiated this process, and ask them to give you honest opinions about how they think it is working, or not working, and what you can do to improve or modify the approach. As is true for other leadership development efforts you may encounter, a constant feedback loop is critical and will keep you on top of things and allow you to recalibrate as needed.

Chapter 9

The End Is the Beginning

So we have come to the end of our book—but it is just the beginning of the journey for you. Throughout the book we have tried to help you discover and understand the "leadership genes" that describe and define your particular style. Hopefully you have gotten a sense of the one or two styles that are most reflective of your natural inclinations. With that understanding, we have given you a number of pragmatic prescriptions you can begin to implement immediately. We've outlined some of the practical realities associated with making the prescriptions work in today's environment. We have done our best to convey that you can achieve all of this without having to change the core of who you are as a person.

Over the course of more than a dozen years, Leadership Solutions has worked with many different leaders to design and implement many different tactics and approaches. We've utilized a wide variety of tools and resources to help leaders improve their personal effectiveness. While all of them have their own unique value, we have found that the prescriptions outlined in this book have yielded the highest unique value for our clients, and continue to benefit them long after we exit the scene.

We've kept in touch with many of our clients even after our formal assignments were completed, keeping track of which prescriptions have led to repeated success. These are the prescriptions outlined in this book. It's gratifying to know that so many of the people who have followed our advice and suggestions have gone on to enhance their careers and become more effective leaders than even they believed they could be. It is because of this that we strongly encourage you to give these prescriptions a try. Most of them are relatively simple to implement and the return you will get is far greater than the effort it will take to put them in place.

That is not to say that you will always get immediate results. Clients who found these prescriptions most meaningful and most impactful are those who trusted us and trusted the process enough to stick with it until results could be measured and analyzed. We all want easy answers (e.g., lose ten pounds by tomorrow; become a millionaire overnight). Yet we know from experience that some of the solutions in this book won't yield results immediately. Structural changes, for example, take time and often take buy-in from other stakeholders. But, like many other things in life, you will find that the time and effort you put in will pay off in the end.

You may think that we are asking you to take a leap of faith. This is true. But we also want you to know that we have faith in you. We have seen over and over again that this process works and we believe that it will work for you as well. It's up to you to make the first move. Don't wait until you have everything perfectly in place—that day will never come.

Before you close this book, ask yourself these five important questions and you will be on your way:

QUESTIONS TO GET YOU STARTED

1. *What is my dominant style? Within that style, what's the most important challenge I face?*
2. *What one or two prescriptions do I think will be most helpful in addressing that challenge?*

3. *Who can help me apply the prescription(s) I have chosen to implement?*
4. *Is there any support or buy-in I need from others in order to get started?*
5. *What one thing in this book can I do differently **today** that will make a difference in my specific situation?*

That's all we're asking of you—do one thing differently today and you'll be amazed at where you find yourself tomorrow. We would love to hear about your journey. We want to know which prescriptions you tried and how your efforts turned out. Perhaps you will be inspired to create your own prescriptions and we would love to know what they are as well.

Feel free to reach out and contact us: send us an email at **info@leadership-solutions.com** and let us know how you're doing.

We wish you all the best!

About the Authors

Dr. **Renee Bellamy Booth** is the founder and president of Leadership Solutions, Inc., a leadership development firm based in Philadelphia since 1999. Prior to founding the firm, she held numerous senior human resource leadership roles in both corporate settings and large international consulting environments. She is an expert in the area of leadership development, having worked with senior level leaders in both small organizations and Fortune 500 corporations, with a specific focus on executive coaching, teambuilding, and leadership assessment. Renee holds her undergraduate degree in Psychology from University of Maryland, and her masters and Ph.D. in Industrial Organizational Psychology from Penn State University.

Michele **A. Porterfield** is a senior consultant with Leadership Solutions, Inc., a leadership development firm based in Philadelphia. Prior to joining the firm when it was founded in 1999, Michele was a consultant with a large international human resources consulting firm in Philadelphia for nine years. Her consulting work specializes in leadership assessment and development as well as executive coaching. She has worked with numerous organizations both large and small, with a particular aim to help individual leaders reach their full potential. Michele has her undergraduate degree from Villanova University and her masters In Organization Development from The American University.

Made in the USA
San Bernardino, CA
24 August 2013